3

Praise for Chocolate Delights
A Collection of Chocolate Recipes
Cookbook Delights Series Book 3

…"If you like eating chocolate as much as I do, then you're going to LOVE *Chocolate Delights Cookbook*! This book is OOZING with hundreds of decadent and delicious recipes that are undeniably savory. *Turtle Toast Royale* and *Double Chocolate Cheesecake* are two of my personal favorites. And, once you try *Chocolate Chili*, you may never again settle for the ordinary! These recipes are rich, versatile, and simple to follow. If you or someone you know is a chocoholic, this cookbook is the cure for your deepest cravings!"…

Kimberly Carter
Chocolate Connoisseur

…"Praise to *Chocolate Delights Cookbook* which has all the makings of a classic favorite. Now you too can prepare that special chocolate dish that everyone wants the recipe for!

Author Karen Jean Matsko Hood presents a wide variety of recipes using chocolate from appetizers to wines and spirits all in organized sections. This book will serve you well through every event, from dinner parties to a quick snack when you, your family and friends are craving something chocolate."…

Ed Archambeault
Spokane, WA

…"Chocolate lovers everywhere will love the depth of information provided in this 324 page cookbook. The information pages and the "*Did You Know? . . . .*" questions provide supportive information to the recipes. This book makes a great gift."…

Dr. James G. Hood
Editor

Praise for Chocolate Delights

A Collection of Chocolate Recipes
Cookbook Delights Series Book 3

…"Chocolate is known to be a mood elevator and a great antioxidant. It is no wonder that **Whispering Pine Press International, Inc.** has included this informational and recipe-packed cookbook to their growing and outstanding collection of *Cookbooks Delights Series.* These well-written and easy-to-follow recipes will be a mouth-watering delight for your family and friends. It's also a great book for dinner parties and special occasions! *Chocolate Delights Cookbook* is a sweet treat for anyone who appreciates one of life's most simple pleasures!"…

Mary Scripture
Graphic Designer

…"When it's cold and frosty outside, there's nothing better than curling up with a nice big mug of homemade hot chocolate. So, why pay several dollars for "gourmet" when you can simply whip up your own delicious drink?

Chocolate Delights Cookbook is the perfect indulgence for anyone who is passionate about the sweet treat. From candies and sauces to main entrées and beverages, this book is drizzled with hundreds of recipe ideas that are sure to please your palate. There is also poetry and fun facts that make it absolutely entertaining to read from cover to cover.

Chocolate lovers, this is the book you've been waiting for!..."

Avid Chocolate Lover
Typist

Chocolate Delights

A Collection of Chocolate Recipes
Cookbook Delights Series Book 3

Karen Jean Matsko Hood

Current and Future Cookbooks
By Karen Jean Matsko Hood

DELIGHTS SERIES

Almond Delights
Anchovy Delights
Apple Delights
Apricot Delights
Artichoke Delights
Asparagus Delights
Avocado Delights
Banana Delights
Barley Delights
Basil Delights
Bean Delights
Beef Delights
Beer Delights
Beet Delights
Blackberry Delights
Blueberry Delights
Bok Choy Delights
Boysenberry Delights
Brazil Nut Delights
Broccoli Delights
Brussels Sprouts Delights
Buffalo Berry Delights
Butter Delights
Buttermilk Delights
Cabbage Delights
Calamari Delights
Cantaloupe Delights
Caper Delights
Cardamom Delights
Carrot Delights
Cashew Delights
Cauliflower Delights
Celery Delights
Cheese Delights
Cherry Delights
Chestnut Delights
Chicken Delights
Chili Pepper Delights
Chive Delights
Chocolate Delights
Chokecherry Delights
Cilantro Delights
Cinnamon Delights
Clam Delights
Clementine Delights
Coconut Delights
Coffee Delights
Conch Delights
Corn Delights
Cottage Cheese Delights
Crab Delights
Cranberry Delights
Cucumber Delights
Cumin Delights
Curry Delights
Date Delights
Edamame Delights
Egg Delights
Eggplant Delights
Elderberry Delights
Endive Delights
Fennel Delights
Fig Delights
Filbert (Hazelnut) Delights
Fish Delights
Garlic Delights
Ginger Delights
Ginseng Delights
Goji Berry Delights
Grape Delights
Grapefruit Delights
Grapple Delights
Guava Delights
Ham Delights
Hamburger Delights
Herb Delights
Herbal Tea Delights
Honey Delights
Honeyberry Delights
Honeydew Delights
Horseradish Delights

Huckleberry Delights
Jalapeño Delights
Jerusalem Artichoke Delights
Jicama Delights
Kale Delights
Kiwi Delights
Kohlrabi Delights
Lavender Delights
Leek Delights
Lemon Delights
Lentil Delights
Lettuce Delights
Lime Delights
Lingonberry Delights
Lobster Delights
Loganberry Delights
Macadamia Nut Delights
Mango Delights
Marionberry Delights
Milk Delights
Mint Delights
Miso Delights
Mushroom Delights
Mussel Delights
Nectarine Delights
Oatmeal Delights
Olive Delights
Onion Delights
Orange Delights
Oregon Berry Delights
Oyster Delights
Papaya Delights
Parsley Delights
Parsnip Delights
Pea Delights
Peach Delights
Peanut Delights
Pear Delights
Pecan Delights
Pepper Delights
Persimmon Delights
Pine Nut Delights
Pineapple Delights
Pistachio Delights
Plum Delights

Pomegranate Delights
Pomelo Delights
Popcorn Delights
Poppy Seed Delights
Pork Delights
Potato Delights
Prickly Pear Cactus Delights
Prune Delights
Pumpkin Delights
Quince Delights
Quinoa Delights
Radish Delights
Raisin Delights
Raspberry Delights
Rhubarb Delights
Rice Delights
Rose Delights
Rosemary Delights
Rutabaga Delights
Salmon Delights
Salmonberry Delights
Salsify Delights
Savory Delights
Scallop Delights
Seaweed Delights
Serviceberry Delights
Sesame Delights
Shallot Delights
Shrimp Delights
Soybean Delights
Spinach Delights
Squash Delights
Star Fruit Delights
Strawberry Delights
Sunflower Seed Delights
Sweet Potato Delights
Swiss Chard Delights
Tangerine Delights
Tapioca Delights
Tayberry Delights
Tea Delights
Teaberry Delights
Thimbleberry Delights
Tofu Delights
Tomatillo Delights

Tomato Delights
Trout Delights
Truffle Delights
Tuna Delights
Turkey Delights
Turmeric Delights
Turnip Delights
Vanilla Delights
Walnut Delights
Wasabi Delights
Watermelon Delights
Wheat Delights
Wild Rice Delights
Yam Delights
Yogurt Delights
Zucchini Delights

CITY DELIGHTS
Chicago Delights
Coeur d'Alene Delights
Great Falls Delights
Honolulu Delights
Minneapolis Delights
Phoenix Delights
Portland Delights
Sandpoint Delights
Scottsdale Delights
Seattle Delights
Spokane Delights
St. Cloud Delights

FOSTER CARE
Foster Care Cookbook
Foster Children Cookbook
  and Activity Book
Foster Children's Favorite
  Recipes
Holiday Cookbook for
  Foster Families

GENERAL THEME
  DELIGHTS
Appetizer Delights
Baby Food Delights
Barbeque Delights
Beer-Making Delights

Beverage Delights
Biscotti Delights
Bisque Delights
Blender Delights
Bread Delights
Bread Maker Delights
Breakfast Delights
Brunch Delights
Cake Delights
Campfire Food Delights
Candy Delights
Canned Food Delights
Cast Iron Delights
Cheesecake Delights
Chili Delights
Chowder Delights
Cocktail Delights
College Cooking Delights
Comfort Food Delights
Cookie Delights
Cooking for One Delights
Cooking for Two Delights
Cracker Delights
Crepe Delights
Crockpot Delights
Dairy Delights
Dehydrated Food Delights
Dessert Delights
Dinner Delights
Dutch Oven Delights
Foil Delights
Fondue Delights
Food Processor Delights
Fried Food Delights
Frozen Food Delights
Fruit Delights
Gelatin Delights
Grilled Delights
Hiking Food Delights
Ice Cream Delights
Juice Delights
Kid's Delights
Kosher Diet Delights
Liqueur-Making Delights
Liqueurs and Spirits Delights

Lunch Delights
Marinade Delights
Microwave Delights
Milk Shake and Malt Delights
Panini Delights
Pasta Delights
Pesto Delights
Phyllo Delights
Pickled Food Delights
Picnic Food Delights
Pizza Delights
Preserved Delights
Pudding and Custard Delights
Quiche Delights
Quick Mix Delights
Rainbow Delights
Salad Delights
Salsa Delights
Sandwich Delights
Sea Vegetable Delights
Seafood Delights
Smoothie Delights
Snack Delights
Soup Delights
Supper Delights
Tart Delights
Torte Delights
Tropical Delights
Vegan Delights
Vegetable Delights
Vegetarian Delights
Vinegar Delights
Wildflower Delights
Wine Delights
Winemaking Delights
Wok Delights

GIFTS-IN-A-JAR SERIES
Beverage Gifts-in-a-Jar
Christmas Gifts-in-a-Jar
Cookie Gifts-in-a-Jar
Gifts-in-a-Jar
Gifts-in-a-Jar Catholic
Gifts-in-a-Jar Christian
Holiday Gifts-in-a-Jar

Soup Gifts-in-a-Jar

HEALTH-RELATED DELIGHTS
Achalasia Diet Delights
Adrenal Health Diet Delights
Anti-Acid Reflux Diet Delights
Anti-Cancer Diet Delights
Anti-Inflammation Diet Delights
Anti-Stress Diet Delights
Arthritis Diet Delights
Bone Health Diet Delights
Diabetic Diet Delights
Fibromyalgia Diet Delights
Gluten-Free Diet Delights
Healthy Breath Diet Delights
Healthy Digestion Diet Delights
Healthy Heart Diet Delights
Healthy Skin Diet Delights
Healthy Teeth Diet Delights
High-Fiber Diet Delights
High-Iodine Diet Delights
High-Protein Diet Delights
Immune Health Diet Delights
Kidney Health Diet Delights
Lactose-Free Diet Delights
Liquid Diet Delights
Liver Health Diet Delights
Low-Calorie Diet Delights
Low-Carb Diet Delights
Low-Fat Diet Delights
Low-Sodium Diet Delights
Low-Sugar Diet Delights
Lymphoma Health Support Diet Delights
Multiple Sclerosis Healthy Diet Delights
No Flour No Sugar Diet Delights
Organic Food Delights
pH-Friendly Diet Delights
Pregnancy Diet Delights
Raw Food Diet Delights

Sjögren's Syndrome Diet
  Delights
Soft Food Diet Delights
Thyroid Health Diet Delights

HOLIDAY DELIGHTS
Christmas Delights
Easter Delights
Father's Day Delights
Fourth of July Delights
Grandparent's Day Delights
Halloween Delights
Hanukkah Delights
Labor Day Weekend Delights
Memorial Day Weekend
  Delights
Mother's Day Delights
New Year's Delights
St. Patrick's Day Delights
Thanksgiving Delights
Valentine Delights

HOOD AND MATSKO
FAMILY FAVORITES
Hood and Matsko Family
  Appetizers Cookbook
Hood and Matsko Family
  Beverages Cookbook
Hood and Matsko Family
  Breads and Rolls Cookbook
Hood and Matsko Family
  Breakfasts Cookbook
Hood and Matsko Family
  Cakes Cookbook
Hood and Matsko Family
  Candies Cookbook
Hood and Matsko Family
  Casseroles Cookbook
Hood and Matsko Family
  Cookies Cookbook
Hood and Matsko Family
  Desserts Cookbook
Hood and Matsko Family
  Dressings, Sauces, and
  Condiments Cookbook

Hood and Matsko Family
  Ethnic Cookbook
Hood and Matsko Family
  Jams, Jellies, Syrups,
  Preserves, and Conserves
Hood and Matsko Family
  Main Dishes Cookbook
Hood and Matsko Family,
  Pies Cookbook
Hood and Matsko Family
  Preserving Cookbook
Hood and Matsko Family
  Salads and Salad Dressings
Hood and Matsko Family
  Side Dishes Cookbook
Hood and Matsko Family
  Vegetable Cookbook
Hood and Matsko Family,
  Aunt Katherine's Recipe
  Collection, Vol. I-II
Hood and Matsko Family,
  Grandma Bert's Recipe
  Collection, Vol. I-IV

HOOD AND MATSKO
FAMILY HOLIDAY
Hood and Matsko Family
  Favorite Birthday Recipes
Hood and Matsko Family
  Favorite Christmas Recipes
Hood and Matsko Family
  Favorite Christmas Sweets
Hood and Matsko Family
  Easter Cookbook
Hood and Matsko Family
  Favorite Thanksgiving Recipes

INTERNATIONAL
DELIGHTS
African Delights
African American Delights
Australian Delights
Austrian Delights
Brazilian Delights
Canadian Delights

Chilean Delights
Chinese Delights
Czechoslovakian Delights
English Delights
Ethiopian Delights
Fijian Delights
French Delights
German Delights
Greek Delights
Hungarian Delights
Icelandic Delights
Indian Delights
Irish Delights
Italian Delights
Korean Delights
Mexican Delights
Native American Delights
Polish Delights
Russian Delights
Scottish Delights
Slovenian Delights
Swedish Delights
Thai Delights
The Netherlands Delights
Yugoslavian Delights
Zambian Delights

REGIONAL DELIGHTS
Glacier National Park Delights
Northwest Regional Delights
Oregon Coast Delights
Schweitzer Mountain Delights
Southwest Regional Delights
Tropical Delights
Washington Wine Country
  Delights
Wine Delights of Walla
  Walla Wineries
Yellowstone National Park
  Delights

SEASONAL DELIGHTS
Autumn Harvest Delights
Spring Harvest Delights
Summer Harvest Delights

Winter Harvest Delights

SPECIAL EVENTS DELIGHTS
Birthday Delights
Coffee Klatch Delights
Super Bowl Delights
Tea Time Delights

STATE DELIGHTS
Alaska Delights
Arizona Delights
Georgia Delights
Hawaii Delights
Idaho Delights
Illinois Delights
Iowa Delights
Louisiana Delights
Minnesota Delights
Montana Delights
North Dakota Delights
Oregon Delights
South Dakota Delights
Texas Delights
Washington Delights

U.S. TERRITORIES DELIGHTS
Cruzan Delights
U.S. Virgin Island Delights

MISCELLANEOUS COOKBOOKS
Getaway Studio Cookbook
The Soup Doctor's Cookbook

BILINGUAL DELIGHTS SERIES
Apple Delights, English-
  French Edition
Apple Delights, English-
  Russian Edition
Apple Delights, English-
  Spanish Edition
Huckleberry Delights,
  English-French Edition

Huckleberry Delights,
English-Russian Edition
Huckleberry Delights,
English-Spanish Edition

CATHOLIC DELIGHTS SERIES
Apple Delights Catholic
Coffee Delights Catholic
Easter Delights Catholic
Huckleberry Delights Catholic
Tea Delights Catholic
Wine Delights Catholic

CATHOLIC BILINGUAL DELIGHTS SERIES
Apple Delights Catholic,
English-French Edition
Apple Delights Catholic,
English-Russian Edition
Apple Delights Catholic,
English-Spanish Edition
Huckleberry Delights
Catholic, English-Spanish
Edition

CHRISTIAN DELIGHTS SERIES
Apple Delights Christian
Coffee Delights Christian
Easter Delights Christian
Huckleberry Delights Christian
Tea Delights Christian
Wine Delights Christian

CHRISTIAN BILINGUAL DELIGHTS SERIES
Apple Delights Christian,
English-French Edition
Apple Delights Christian,
English-Russian Edition
Apple Delights Christian,
English-Spanish Edition
Huckleberry Delights
Christian, English-Spanish
Edition

FUNDRAISING COOKBOOKS
Ask about our fundraising
cookbooks to help raise
funds for your organization.

The above books are also available in bilingual versions. Please contact Whispering Pine Press International, Inc., for details.

Please note that some books are future books and are currently in production. Please contact us for availability date. Prices are subject to change without notice.

The above list of books is not all-inclusive. For a complete list please visit our website or contact us at:

Whispering Pine Press International, Inc.
Your Northwest Book Publishing Company
P.O. Box 214
Spokane Valley, WA 99037-0214 USA
Phone: (509) 928-8700 | Fax: (509) 922-9949
Email: sales@whisperingpinepress.com
Publisher Websites: www.WhisperingPinePress.com
www.WhisperingPinePressBookstore.com
Blog: www.WhisperingPinePressBlog.com

Chocolate Delights

A Collection of Chocolate Recipes
Cookbook Delights Series Book 3

Karen Jean Matsko Hood

Published by:

Whispering Pine Press International, Inc.
Your Northwest Book Publishing Company
P.O. Box 214
Spokane Valley, WA 99037-0214 USA
Phone: (509) 928-8700 | Fax: (509) 922-9949
Email: sales@whisperingpinepress.com
Websites: www.WhisperingPinePress.com
www.WhisperingPinePressBookstore.com
Blog: www.WhisperingPinePressBlog.com
SAN 253-200X
Printed in the U.S.A

Published by Whispering Pine Press International, Inc.
P.O. Box 214
Spokane Valley, Washington 99037-0214 USA

For sales outside the United States, please contact the Whispering Pine Press International, Inc., International Sales Department.

Manufactured in the United States of America. This paper is acid-free and 100% chlorine free.

Book and Cover Design by Artistic Design Service, Inc.
P.O. Box 1782
Spokane Valley, WA 99037-1782 USA
www.ArtisticDesignService.com

Library of Congress Number (LCCN): 2014901589

Hood, Karen Jean Matsko
    Title: Chocolate Delights, A Collection of Chocolate Recipes: ·
Cookbook Delights Series Book 3

    p.   cm.

ISBN: 978-1-59649-120-5   case bound
ISBN: 978-1-59649-121-2   perfect bound
ISBN: 978-1-59649-122-9   spiral bound
ISBN: 978-1-59649-123-6   comb bound
ISBN: 978-1-59649-125-0   E-PDF
ISBN: 978-1-59210-387-4   E-PUB
ISBN: 978-1-59434-861-7   E-PRC

First Edition: January 2014
1. Cookery (Chocolate Delights : A Collection of Chocolate Recipes: *Cookbook Delights Series* Book 3)   1. Title

Chocolate Delights

A Collection of Chocolate Recipes
Cookbook Delights Series Book 3

Gift Inscription

To:_____

From: _____

Date: _____

Special Message: _____

_____

_____

_____

_____

_____

_____

_____

_____

*It is always nice to receive a personal note to
create a special memory.*

www.ChocolateDelights.us
www.WhisperingPinePress.com
www.WhisperingPinePressBookstore.com

Dedications

To my husband and best friend, Jim.

To our seventeen children: Gabriel, Brianne Kristina and her husband Moulik Vinodkumar Kothari, Marissa Kimberly and her husband Kevin Matthew Franck, Janelle Karina and her husband Paul Joseph Turcotte, Mikayla Karlene, Kyler James, Kelsey Katrina, Corbin Joel, Caleb Jerome, Keisha Kalani Hiwot, Devontay Joshua, Kianna Karielle Selam, Rosy Kiara, Mercedes Katherine, Jasmine Khalia Wengel, Cheyenne Krystal, and Annalise Kaylee Marie.

To our grandchildren and foster grandchildren: Courtney, Lorenzo, and Leah.

To my brother, Stephen, and his wife, Karen.

To my husband's ten siblings: Gary, Colleen, John, Dan, Mary, Ray, Ann, Teresa, Barbara, Agnes, and their families.

In loving memory of my mom, who passed away in 2007; my dad, who passed away in 1976; and my sister, Sandy, who passed away due to multiple sclerosis in 1999.

To Sandy's three sons: Monte, Bradley, and Derek. To Monte's wife, Sarah, and their children: Liam, Alice, Charlie, and Samuel and their foster children. To Bradley's wife, Shawnda, and their children: Anton, Isaac, and Isabel.

To our foster children past and present: Krystal, Sara, Rebecca, Janice, Devontay Joshua, Mercedes Katherine, Zha'Nell, Makia, Onna, Cheyenne Krystal, Onna Marie, Nevaeh, and Zada, our future foster children, and all foster children everywhere.

To the Court Appointed Special Advocate (CASA) Volunteer Program in the judicial system which benefits abused and neglected children.

To the Literacy Campaign dedicated to promoting literacy throughout the world.

Acknowledgements

I would like to acknowledge all those individuals who helped me during the time I wrote this book. I appreciate all the time and effort they put into this project.

I owe deep gratitude and profound thanks to my husband, Jim, for giving freely of his time and encouragement during this project. Also, I owe thanks to my children Gabriel, Brianne Kristina and her husband Moulik Kothari, Marissa Kimberly, Janelle Karina and her husband Paul Turcotte, Mikayla Karlene, Kyler James, Kelsey Katrina, Corbin Joel, Caleb Jerome, Keisha Kalani, Devontay Joshua, Kianna Karielle, Rosy Kiara, Mercedes Katherine, Jasmine Khalia, Cheyenne Krystal, and Anna Kaylee. They all inspire my writing.

I wish to thank Carol Spitzer and Sharron Thompson for their assistance in typing this manuscript for publication. Thank you to Allyson Schnabel for the final proofing of this manuscript for publication and to Artistic Design Service, Inc. for their assistance in formatting and providing a graphic design of this manuscript for publication. This project could not have been completed without them.

A great many thanks are due to my family, all of whom were very supportive during the time it took to complete this project. Their patience and support are greatly appreciated.

Chocolate Delights

Table of Contents

Chocolate Delights
A Collection of Chocolate Recipes
Cookbook Delights Series Book 3

Introduction

Chocolate has always been one of my favorite survival foods. It is full of addictive flavor and popular in all forms of preparation. It is great for cooking and wonderful to eat any time of the day or night. If you have never seen the blossoms of the cacao tree, they are beautiful. If you do not have access to a computer, please check with your local library to find pictures of this beautiful tree.

As a poet, I found it enjoyable to color this cookbook with poetry so that readers could savor the metaphorical richness of chocolate as well as its literal flavor. Also included are some articles on history, cultivation, and botanical information, along with interesting facts about chocolate. Sections that discuss health and nutrition as well as some chocolate folklore are also included in this book.

The *Cookbook Delights Series* would not be complete without *Chocolate Delights Cookbook, Volume I,* since chocolates are such a prized American treat. We hope you enjoy reading this cookbook as well as trying out all of the delicious recipes that have been gathered together for your culinary adventures.

The cookbook is organized in convenient alphabetical sections to assist you in finding recipes related to the type of cooking you need: appetizers and dips; beverages; breads and rolls; breakfasts; cakes; candies; cookies; desserts; dressings, sauces, and condiments; jams, jellies, and syrups; main dishes; pies; preserving; salads; side dishes; soups; and wines and spirits.

Following is a collection of information and recipes gathered and modified to bring you *Chocolate Delights Cookbook, Volume I: A Collection of Chocolate Recipes, Cookbook Delights Series* by Karen Jean Matsko Hood.

Chocolate Delights
A Collection of Chocolate Recipes
Cookbook Delights Series Book 3

Chocolate Botanical Classification

Chocolate Botanical Classification

Kingdom: *Plantae*
Division: *Magnoliophyta*
Class: *Magnoliopsida*
Order: *Malvales*
Family: *Sterculiaceae*
Genus: *Theobroma*
Species: *T. cacao*
Binomial Name: *Theobroma cacao*

Chocolate is a flavoring made from the seeds of the cacao tree. The cacao is a small 15 to 26-foot evergreen tree in the family Sterculiaceae (alternatively Malvaceae), native to the deep tropical region of South America. Its seeds are used to produce cocoa butter, the chocolate drink, as well as chocolate. Nowadays the trees are grown in plantations in many tropical countries.

There are two prominent competing theories about the origins of the original wild *Theobroma* cacao tree. One group of proponents believe wild examples were originally distributed from southeastern Mexico to the Amazon basin, with domestication taking place both in the Lacandon area of Mesoamerica and in lowland South America. Recent studies of *Theobroma* cacao genetics seem to show that the plant originated in the Amazon and was distributed by man throughout Central America and Mesoamerica.

The bush is today found growing wild in the low foothills of the Andes at elevations of around 650 to 1300 feet in the Amazon and Orinoco river basins. It requires a humid climate with regular rainfall and good soil. It is an understory tree, growing best with some overhead shade. The leaves are alternate, entire, unlobed, 4 to 16 inches long and 2 to 8 inches broad.

Chocolate Delights
A Collection of Chocolate Recipes
Cookbook Delights Series Book 3

Chocolate (Cacao) Cultivation

Chocolate (Cacao) Cultivation

Cacao is planted on over 70,000 square kilometers worldwide with 40% of production coming from Côte d'Ivoire, Ghana, and Indonesia. Each country produces about 15%, with smaller amounts coming from Brazil, Nigeria, and Cameroon.

A tree begins to bear fruit when it is 4 or 5 years old. In one year, when mature, it may have 6,000 flowers, but only about 20 pods. About 300 to 600 seeds (10 pods) are required to produce around 1 kg of cocoa paste.

The cacao flowers are produced in clusters directly on the trunk and older branches. They are small, ½ to 1 inch in diameter, with pink calyx. While many of the world's flowers are pollinated by bees or butterflies/moths, cacao flowers are pollinated by tiny flies, midges in the order Diptera.

The fruit, called a cacao pod, is ovoid, 6 to 12 inches long and 3 to 4 inches wide, ripening yellow to orange, and weighs about 1 pound when ripe. The pod contains 20 to 60 seeds, usually called "beans", embedded in a white pulp. Each seed contains a significant amount of fat (40 to 50% as cocoa butter). Their most noted active constituent is *Theobromine*, a compound similar but different from caffeine.

There are three main cultivar groups of cacao beans used to make cocoa and chocolate.

1. The most prized, rare, and expensive is the Criollo group, the cocoa bean used by the Maya. Only 10% of chocolate is made from the Criollo, which is less bitter and more aromatic than any other bean.
2. The cacao bean in 80% of chocolate is made using beans of the Forastero group. Forastero trees are significantly hardier than Criollo trees, resulting in cheaper cacao beans.
3. Trinitario, a hybrid of Criollo and Forastero, is used in about 10% of chocolate.

Chocolate Delights
A Collection of Chocolate Recipes
Cookbook Delights Series Book 3

Chocolate Facts

Chocolate Facts

Cacao beans were commonly used as currency in Pre-Columbian Mesoamerica. In some areas, such as Yucatán, they were still used in place of small coins as late as the 1840s.

The definition of chocolate: At the core of the chocolate debate across Europe, parts of Asia, and the United States is the definition of chocolate itself, and whether percentages of cocoa in production should render some candies unable to carry the chocolate food definition. Currently the United States, the European Union, and Russia do not allow vegetable fats as ingredients of products labeled as chocolate.

At issue also is the ability to replace cocoa butter or dairy components of chocolate with cheaper vegetable fats or PGPR, thereby reducing the quantity of actual cocoa in the finished product while creating an arguably more unhealthy confection.

So, is "white chocolate" really chocolate? White chocolate is a misnomer. Under Federal Standards of Identity, real chocolate must contain chocolate liquor. "White" chocolate contains no chocolate liquor.

Is chocolate an aphrodisiac? Not really. Chocolate contains small amounts of a chemical called *phenyl ethylamine* (PEA), which is a mild mood elevator. That is the same chemical that our brain produces when we feel happy or "in love."

Chocolate aroma for relaxation. One study has shown that the smell of chocolate may actually relax you by increasing theta waves in the brain.

Caffeine in chocolate. There is probably not enough caffeine in chocolate to make you jittery. Cacao does contain a number of stimulants, such as caffeine and *Theobromine*, but in small amounts that are diluted even further when processed into chocolate. In fact, one ounce of milk chocolate contains about the same amount of caffeine as one cup of decaffeinated coffee.

Chocolate Delights
A Collection of Chocolate Recipes
Cookbook Delights Series Book 3

Chocolate Folklore

Chocolate (Cacao) Folklore

The Maya believed that the kakaw (cacao) was discovered by the gods in a mountain that also contained other delectable foods to be used by the Maya. According to Maya mythology, the Plumed Serpent gave cacao to the Maya after humans were created from maize by divine grandmother goddess Xmucane.

The Maya celebrated an annual festival in April to honor their cacao god, Ek Chuah, an event that included the sacrifice of a dog with cacao-colored markings; additional animal sacrifices; offerings of cacao, feathers, and incense; and an exchange of gifts.

In a similar creation story, the Mexican (Aztec) god Quetzalcoatl discovered cacao (*cacahuatl*: bitter water), in a mountain filled with other plant foods. Cacao was offered regularly to a pantheon of Mexican deities and the Madrid Codex depicts priests lancing their ear lobes (autosacrifice) and covering the cacao with blood as a suitable sacrifice to the gods. The cacao beverage as ritual were used only by men, as it was believed to be toxic for women and children.

There are several mixtures of cacao described in ancient texts, for ceremonial, medicinal uses as well as culinary purposes. Some mixtures included maize, chili, vanilla, peanut butter, and honey. Archaeological evidence for use of cacao, while relatively sparse, has come from the recovery of whole cacao beans in Guatemala and from the preservation of wood fragments of the cacao tree at Belize sites. In addition, analysis of residues from ceramic vessels has found traces of *Theobromine* and caffeine in early formative vessels from Puerto Escondido, Honduras (1100 to 900 B.C.), and in middle formative vessels from Colha, Belize (600 to 400 B.C.) using similar techniques to those used to extract chocolate residues from four classic period (400 A.D.) vessels from a tomb at the archaeological site of Rio Azul.

As cacao is the only known commodity from Mesoamerica containing both of these alkaloid compounds, it seems likely that these vessels were used as containers for cacao drinks.

Chocolate Delights
A Collection of Chocolate Recipes
Cookbook Delights Series Book 3

Chocolate History

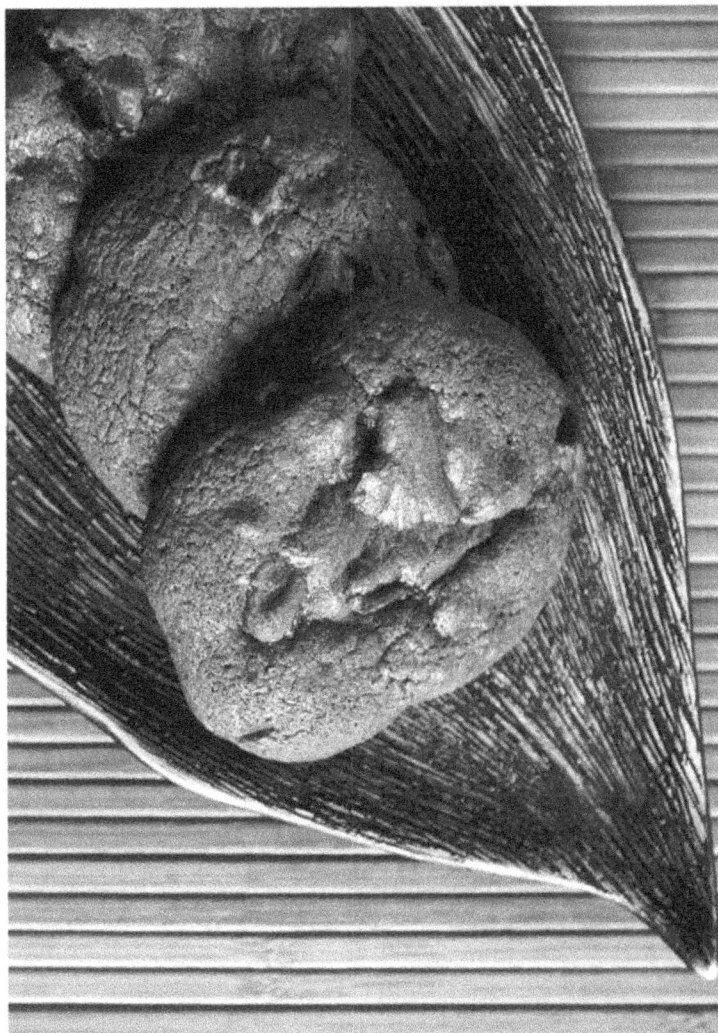

History of the Cacao Tree

Cultivation, cultural elaboration, and use of cacao were extensive in Mesoamerica. Studies of the *Theobroma cacao* tree genetics suggests a domestication and spread from lowland Amazonia, contesting an earlier hypothesis that the tree was domesticated independently in both the Lacandon area of Mexico and in Amazonia.

The cacao tree belongs to the *Theobroma* genus, in the *Sterculiaceae* family, that contains 22 species. Today, the most common of the cultivated species is *Theobroma cacao*, with two subspecies and three forms. Wild cacaos fall into two groups. The South American subspecies *spaerocarpum* has a fairly smooth melon-like fruit. In contrast, the Mesoamerican cacao subspecies has ridged, elongated fruits. At some unknown early date, the subspecies *T. cacao* reached the southern lowlands of Mesoamerica and came into wide usage.

The first Europeans to encounter cacao were Christopher Columbus and his crew in 1502, when they captured a canoe at Guanaja that contained a quantity of mysterious-looking "almonds." They at first mistook them for rabbit droppings.

The first real European knowledge about chocolate came in the form of a beverage that was first introduced to the Spanish at their meeting with Montezuma in the Aztec capital of Tenochtitlan in 1519. Cortez and others noted the vast quantities of this beverage that the Aztec emperor consumed and how it was carefully whipped by his attendants beforehand.

Examples of cacao beans along with other agricultural products were brought back to Spain at that time; but it seems that the beverage made from cacao was introduced to the Spanish court in 1544 by Kekchi Maya nobles, brought from the New World to Spain by Dominican friars to meet Prince Philip.

Within a century, the culinary and medical uses of chocolate had spread to France, England, and elsewhere in Western Europe. Demand for this beverage led the French to establish cacao plantations in the Caribbean, while Spain subsequently developed their cacao plantations in their Philippine colony.

Chocolate Delights
A Collection of Chocolate Recipes
Cookbook Delights Series Book 3

Chocolate Nutrition and Health

Chocolate Nutrition and Health

Cocoa drinks and chocolate contain an abundant dose of *flavonoids*, potent antioxidants that have been found most notably in green tea, red wine, and fruits and vegetables. Higher anti-oxidants have been associated with a decrease in the risk of coronary heart disease and stroke by cutting cholesterol levels.

Research has found that chocolate carries high levels of chemicals known as *phenolics*, some of which may help lower the risk of heart disease.

Ten percent of U.S. Recommended Daily Allowance of iron is found in one ounce of baking chocolate or cocoa. Chocolate also contains Vitamins A1, B1, B2, C, D, and E, as well as calcium, potassium, sodium, and iron.

The American Heart Association recommends that daily cholesterol intake not exceed 300 mg. A chocolate bar is actually low in cholesterol. A 1.65-oz. bar contains only 12 mg. A one-ounce piece of Cheddar cheese contains 30 mg. of cholesterol - more than double the amount found in a chocolate bar.

Chocolate, often referred to as the "feel good food," contains more than 300 known chemicals. Scientists have been working on isolating specific chemicals and chemical combinations that can explain the pleasurable sensation chocolate provides. Caffeine is the most known chemical found in chocolate. While the caffeine in chocolate is small, *Theobromine*, a weak stimulant, is also present. Scientists believe that perhaps the combination of these stimulants and others may be responsible for the "boost" that chocolate eaters experience.

Phyenykethkamine is also found in chocolate. This chemical occurs naturally in the brain and is related to amphetamines. The combination of these stimulants increases the activity of brain chemicals, neurotransmitters that enable the body to pay attention and be alert.

Chocolate Delights
A Collection of Chocolate Recipes
Cookbook Delights Series Book 3

Poetry

A Collection of Poetry with Chocolate Themes

Table of Contents

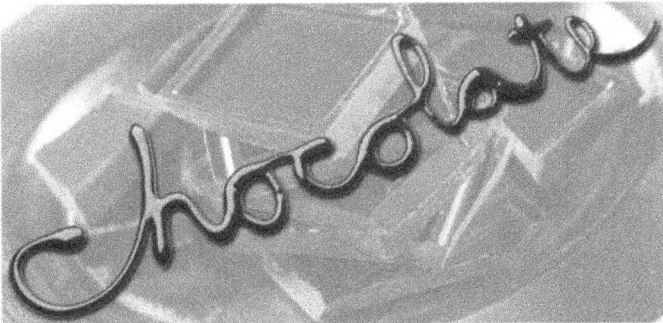

Afternoon Chocolate

Nothing is as lovely
as a smooth velvety
cup of hot chocolate
topped with marshmallows
melted just so.

Memories of fragrant
chocolate cooking on the stove
as the patter of little
feet run through open doors
to warm their cold hands on a
soothing cup of hot chocolate.

Karen Jean Matsko Hood ©2014
Published in *Chocolate Delights,* 2014
By Whispering Pine Press International, Inc., 2014

Chocolate Memories

Brick framed the fireplace
with brass doors under
a chimney mantle.

Children played cards by the
warmth of the fire and the home was filled
with the essence of chocolate
melted on the stove.

Karen Jean Matsko Hood ©2014
Published in *Chocolate Delights,* 2014
By Whispering Pine Press International, Inc., 2014

Brown Eyes

I remember his toffee eyes,
friendly and warm,
full of life,
looking for fun.
Don't forget the smile,
that Cheshire-cat smirk.

Mischievous,
sensuous, lips
yearn to give.
Encore the brown eyes,
relaxed, affectionate,
ready to love,
to give again.

Memories abound,
his tender chocolate eyes,
soft lips of crimson.
How I miss his smile,
that impetuous grin,
the wish of a tender kiss.

Karen Jean Matsko Hood ©2014
Published in *Chocolate Delights,* 2014
By Whispering Pine Press International, Inc., 2014

Coco's Bakery

Have you ever driven to Spokane, Washington?
That quaint place in the mountains,
an eclectic mix of cultures.
Academics, aging flower children,
University professors, fresh-faced students.

All work to earn a mark, to yield a difference.
Culinary cuisine, epicurean delights,
combine to build patchwork landscape
old and new, bakers and chefs,
epicureans and connoisseurs.

Quintessential spiced chocolate and cocoa
soaked with the aroma of java
and ground coffee beans, fancy latte's and
buttery homemade pastries.

I prefer the warm hot chocolate
served with marshmallows melted.
Sweet treats melt in my mouth,
as I watch the wonderful
brought before my curious eyes.

Karen Jean Matsko Hood ©2014
Published in *Chocolate Delights,* 2014
By Whispering Pine Press International, Inc., 2014

Chocolate Delights

Chocolate delights bring dreams
Home around the holidays
Of candies, fudge, pies, and all three
Chocolate. Cakes made from scratch
Of imported cocoa. Bittersweet
Latte's decorated with whipped cream dollops
All colors of chocolate decorate the
Table as family and guests
Enthusiastically welcome the seasoned food.

Delectable main dishes and scrumptious desserts
Enliven the meal as conversations contend.
Light dims as night arrives.
Incandescent candles flicker and
Glow in brass lanterns to illuminate
Homes that swell with holiday guests.
Tradition welcomes the bounty of food rich with
Sweet chocolate delights.

Karen Jean Matsko Hood ©2014
Published in *Chocolate Delights,* 2014
By Whispering Pine Press International, Inc., 2014

Spilled Chocolate and Night Memories

Chocolate spilled on the lace tablecloth
reminds me of you,

those fine meals we shared
alone together in front of the fireplace.

We slowly sipped wine as we
savored our gourmet menu.

Classical music serenaded
us in the hushed background of mountain peaks.

Fragrant carnations perfume the air,
rich chocolate, sweet symphony.

Succulent rose blossoms by candlelight.
How delightful are the reminders of you.

Karen Jean Matsko Hood ©2014
Published in *Chocolate Delights,* 2014
By Whispering Pine Press International, Inc., 2014

Tropical Garden

Do you remember the view of
that tropical summer garden?
Dark rich cocoa beans
hung as tiny ornaments
on the verdant tree.

Night sounds, incredible music.
You felt a crunch in clumps
under the soles of your
playful, stumbling tread.

Bountiful flowers swayed with
bright saffron centers behind
grandstand hues of orchids.
Honeybees, multi-tasking nectar-makers,
gathered golden pollen.

Topaz-yellow velvet,
quiet under purple,
Fragrant cocoa beans
oh, that tropical garden
I do miss.

Karen Jean Matsko Hood ©2014
Published in *Chocolate Delights,* 2014
By Whispering Pine Press International, Inc., 2014

Toast

Blown crystal glass velvety chocolate
We toast together,
And share the fire
As we sit side by side,
Fireside chats by candlelight
Warm thoughts
Soothing chocolate
and memories of you.

Karen Jean Matsko Hood ©2014
Published in *Chocolate Delights,* 2014
By Whispering Pine Press International, Inc., 2014

Chocolate Dreams

Can you see the snow clouds that drift overhead
High above the snow-capped mountain peaks,
Over blue hills, between verdant valleys?
Childhood memories abound with
Occasions of birthdays, holidays, and more.
Loved ones remembered,
Always a celebration around the
Table, always an extra chair for
Each surprise guest.

Delicious baked goodies from Grandma's oven
Remembered in the best of dreams
Everything you ever wanted
Amid loving air and fragrant spices.
Mom helping as children look on with delight,
Sweet dreams, memories of families,
    grandma's home baked chocolate dreams.

Karen Jean Matsko Hood ©2014
Published in *Chocolate Delights,* 2014
By Whispering Pine Press International, Inc., 2014

Childhood Memories

Rich chocolate ice cream drips down ceramic dishes,
cocoa textures piled high and
perched upon woven waffle cones.

Children grab while grandparents wait.
Chocolate candy twists and spirals on
toffee mounds that punctuate ice crystals.

Delicious chocolate memories, the rich
display of colors, fragrant in
childhood minds.

Karen Jean Matsko Hood ©2014
Published in *Chocolate Delights,* 2014
By Whispering Pine Press International, Inc., 2014

Chocolate Delights
A Collection of Chocolate Recipes
Cookbook Delights Series Book 3

Chocolate Types

Chocolate Types

The cacao bean products from which chocolate is made are known under different names in different parts of the world. In the American chocolate industry:

- Chocolate liquor is the ground or melted state of the nib of the cacao bean.
- Cocoa butter is the fat component.
- Cocoa powder is the nonfat part of the cacao bean that is ground into a powder.

Types of Chocolate

product	chocolate liquor	milk solids	sugar
milk chocolate	$\geq 10\%$	$\geq 12\%$	
sweet chocolate	≥ 15	$< 12\%$	
semi-sweet or bittersweet (dark) chocolate	≥ 35	$< 12\%$	
white chocolate	$\geq 20\%$	$\geq 14\%$	$\leq 55\%$

Chocolate is a popular ingredient and is available in many types. Different forms and flavors of chocolate are produced by varying the quantities of the different ingredients.

Other flavors can be obtained by varying the time and temperature when roasting the beans.

Unsweetened chocolate is pure chocolate liquor, also known as bitter or baking chocolate. It is unadulterated chocolate: the pure, ground, roasted chocolate beans impart a strong, deep chocolate flavor. With the addition of sugar, however, it is used as the base for cakes, brownies, confections, and cookies.

Dark chocolate is chocolate without milk as an additive. It is sometimes called "plain chocolate." The U.S. Government calls this "sweet chocolate" and requires a 15 percent concentration of chocolate liquor. European rules specify a minimum of 35 percent cocoa solids.

Milk chocolate is chocolate with milk powder or condensed milk added. The U.S. Government requires a 10 percent concentration of chocolate liquor. European Union regulations specify a minimum of 25 percent cocoa solids.

Semi-sweet chocolate is often used for cooking purposes. It is a dark chocolate with a low (typically half) sugar content.

Bittersweet chocolate is chocolate liquor (or unsweetened chocolate) to which some sugar (typically a third), more cocoa butter, vanilla, and sometimes lecithin have been added. It has less sugar and more liquor than semi-sweet chocolate, but the two are interchangeable in baking. Bittersweet and semi-sweet chocolates are sometimes referred to as "couverture" (chocolate that contains at least 32 percent cocoa butter). Many brands now print on the package the percentage of cocoa (as chocolate liquor and added cocoa butter) contained. The rule is that the higher the percentage of cocoa, the less sweet the chocolate will be.

Couverture is a term used for chocolates rich in cocoa butter. Popular brands of couverture used by professional pastry chefs and often sold in gourmet and specialty food stores include: Valrhona, Felchlin, Lindt and Sprüngli, Scharffen Berger, Cacao Barry, Callebaut, and Guittard.

These chocolates contain a high percentage of cocoa (sometimes 70 percent or more) and have a total fat content of 30 to 40 percent.

White chocolate is a confection based on cocoa butter without the cocoa solids.

Cocoa powder has two types of unsweetened baking cocoa available: natural cocoa (like the sort produced by Hershey's and Nestlé) and Dutch-process cocoa (such as the Hershey's European Style Cocoa and the Droste brand). Both are made by pulverizing partially defatted chocolate liquor and removing nearly all the cocoa butter. Natural cocoa is light in color and somewhat acidic with a strong chocolate flavor. Natural cocoa is commonly used in recipes which call for baking soda. Because baking soda is an alkali, combining it with natural cocoa creates a leavening action that allows the batter to rise during baking. Dutch-process cocoa is processed with alkali to neutralize its natural acidity. Dutch cocoa is slightly milder in taste, with a deeper and warmer color than natural cocoa. Dutch-process cocoa is frequently used for chocolate drinks such as hot chocolate due to its ease in blending with liquids. Unfortunately, Dutch processing destroys most of the flavonols present in cocoa.

Compound chocolate is the technical term for a confection combining cocoa with vegetable fat, usually tropical fats and/or hydrogenated fats, as a replacement for cocoa butter. It is primarily used for candy bar coatings; but because it does not contain cocoa butter, in the U.S. it is not allowed to be called "chocolate." Unfortunately in America, to the untrained observer the adjective used for this substance appears to merely be the adjectival form of chocolate: "chocolaty." The candy bars sold in America often no longer have true chocolate as a major component. This is especially true for much candy passed as "white chocolate", which need not contain anything from the cacao bush at all. This can translate to poor taste, texture, and possibly health concerns, particularly when partially hydrogenated oils are used to replace cacao butter.

Chocolate Delights
A Collection of Chocolate Recipes
Cookbook Delights Series Book 3

RECIPES

Chocolate Delights

A Collection of Chocolate Recipes
Cookbook Delights Series Book 3

Appetizers and Dips

Table of Contents

Page

Chocolate Candy Bar Fondue

This makes a delicious and rich chocolate appetizer or dessert that can be made ahead of time and reheated when ready to use.

Ingredients:

    5   med. chocolate candy bars
    1   c. heavy whipping cream
    2   Tbs. corn syrup
    ¼   c. brandy
    12 lg. fresh, whole strawberries, rinsed, stems intact

Directions:

1. Break and melt candy bars in top of double boiler.
2. Stirring continuously, add the cream.
3. Immediately add corn syrup and keep stirring; turn off heat.
4. Cover until ready to serve.
5. When ready to serve, place strawberries on a tray and serve beside the fondue pot.

Chili Mole Popcorn

This mole popcorn makes an interesting snack or appetizer.

Ingredients:

    1   Tbs. chili powder
    1   tsp. unsweetened cocoa powder
    1   tsp. vegetable seasoning
    1   tsp. salt
    ¼   tsp. black pepper, freshly ground
    8   c. hot popcorn
        cooking spray, butter-flavored

Directions:

1. In small bowl, combine chili powder, cocoa, vegetable seasoning, salt, and pepper.
2. Lightly spray the sides of a large serving bowl with butter-flavored spray.
3. Add 2 or 3 cups of hot popcorn.
4. Spray lightly and sprinkle evenly with a heaping teaspoon of mixed seasonings.
5. Add another layer of popcorn, spray, and seasoning mixture.
6. Add a final layer of popcorn and spray, and sprinkle remaining seasoning over everything.
7. Serve at once without tossing.

Yields: 8 cups popcorn.

Chocolate Dipped Strawberries

These make a very attractive dessert. Our family really enjoys chocolate-covered strawberries with or without the liqueur or brandy for extra flavor.

Ingredients:

2   Tbs. butter
2   tsp. cognac, or brandy, or orange liqueur (optional)
24 lg. strawberries, stems attached.
6   oz. semi-sweet chocolate

Directions:

1. Melt chocolate in double boiler over hot water, or in microwave oven.
2. Dip strawberries halfway into chocolate and set on a plate covered with a sheet of wax paper.
3. Refrigerate 10 minutes, or just long enough for the chocolate to set.
4. Eat them the day you make them.

Chocolate Plunge Dip

This warm, rich, and creamy dip is delicious.

Ingredients:

⅔ c. white corn syrup
½ c. heavy cream
1 pkg. semi-sweet chocolate chips (8 oz.)

Directions:

1. In medium saucepan, stir syrup and cream.
2. Over medium-high heat, bring to boil.
3. Remove from heat, add chocolate; stir until melted.
4. To serve, keep warm.

Chocolate Chip Cheese Ball

This is a great recipe to use when you need a unique appetizer for a potluck, or it can be used as an afternoon snack, or at a brunch.

Ingredients:

1 pkg. cream cheese, softened (8 oz.)
½ c. butter, softened
¼ tsp. vanilla extract
¾ c. powdered sugar
2 Tbs. brown sugar
¾ c. semi-sweet chocolate chips, miniature
¾ c. pecans, finely chopped
　 graham crackers

Directions:

1. In mixing bowl, with electric mixer, beat cream cheese, butter, and vanilla until fluffy.

2. Gradually add sugars; beat just until combined.
3. Stir in chocolate chips.
4. Cover; refrigerate 2 hours.
5. Place cream cheese mixture on a large piece of plastic wrap; shape into a ball.
6. Refrigerate 1 hour.
7. Just before serving, roll cheese ball in pecans.
8. Serve with graham crackers, or chocolate, or vanilla wafers.

Fruit and Coffee Fondue

This yummy fondue blends the flavors of caramel, chocolate, coffee, and apples. Enjoy.

Ingredients:

1 lb. caramel candies (16 oz.)
¼ c. milk
⅓ c. strongly brewed coffee
½ c. milk chocolate or dark chocolate chips
2 lg. Granny Smith or Macintosh apples, cut into cubes
1 doz. marshmallows, cut in half

Directions:

1. Boil water in bottom of double boiler, then add caramels, milk, coffee, and chocolate chips to top pan and heat.
2. Stir until all ingredients are melted and well blended.
3. Slowly and carefully pour into fondue pot and light heating element under it.
4. Serve with a platter of fruit and marshmallows.
5. Note: Fresh pineapple, pears, and strawberries are delicious alternatives.

Yields: 4 servings.

Chocolate Cream Fruit Dip

This dip is a nice change of pace from the traditional vegetable/dip trays. Try it when you want something light and refreshing.

Ingredients:

> 1 pkg. cream cheese, softened (8 oz.)
> ¼ c. chocolate syrup
> 1 jar marshmallow crème
>   fresh strawberries

Directions:

> 1. In a small mixing bowl, beat cream cheese and chocolate syrup together.
> 2. Fold in marshmallow crème.
> 3. Cover and refrigerate until serving time.
> 4. Serve with fruit.

Yields: 2 cups.

Chocolate Dipped Appetizers

Chocolate-covered salty pretzels provide some variety for your appetizer tray.

Ingredients:

> ½ c. milk chocolate chips
> ½ c. semi-sweet chocolate chips
> 1 Tbs. shortening (no substitutions)
>   miniature pretzels, bagel chips, or dried apricots

Directions:

1. Cover tray with wax paper.
2. Place chocolate chips and shortening in small, microwave-safe bowl.
3. Microwave on high 1 minute; stir.
4. If necessary, microwave on high an additional 15 seconds at a time, stirring after each heating, just until chips are melted and mixture is smooth when stirred.
5. Cool slightly.
6. Dip ⅔ of each snack or fruit into chocolate mixture.
7. Shake gently to remove excess chocolate.
8. Place on prepared tray.
9. Refrigerate, uncovered, about 30 minutes or until coating is firm.
10. Store in airtight container in cool, dry place.

Yields: ½ cup.

Chocolate Orange Dip

This dip is so easy to make, and you will enjoy the orange and chocolate combination.

Ingredients:

6　Tbs. plain yogurt
6　Tbs. prepared chocolate sauce
1½ tsp. frozen orange juice concentrate, thawed

Directions:

1. In small bowl, combine yogurt, chocolate fudge sauce, and orange juice concentrate.
2. Mix well.
3. Chill before serving.

Chocolate Peanut Butter Dipped Apples

Here is a tasty alternative from the usual caramel covered apples, which are delicious also. Try this chocolate peanut butter variety.

Ingredients:

> 12 med. apples, stems removed
> 12 wooden ice cream sticks
> 1   c. semi-sweet chocolate chips
> 1⅔ c. peanut butter chips, divided (10 oz.)
> ¼   c. plus 2 Tbs. shortening, divided (no substitutions)

Directions:

1. Line tray with wax paper.
2. Wash apples; dry thoroughly.
3. Insert wooden stick into stem end of each apple; place on prepared tray.
4. Place chocolate chips, ⅔ cup peanut butter chips, and ¼ cup shortening in medium microwave-safe bowl.
5. Microwave on high for 1 minute; stir.
6. If necessary, microwave on high an additional 30 seconds at a time, stirring after each heating, just until chips are melted when stirred.
7. Dip bottom ¾ of each apple into mixture.
8. Twirl and gently shake to remove excess; return to prepared tray.
9. Place remaining peanut butter chips and remaining shortening in small microwave-safe bowl.
10. Microwave on high for 30 seconds; stir.
11. If necessary, microwave on high an additional 15 seconds at a time, stirring after each heating, just until chips are melted when stirred.
12. Spoon over top section of each apple; allow to drip down sides.
13. Refrigerate until ready to serve.

Chocolate Cream Cheese Dip

This makes a unique cream cheese dip that will delight your guests.

Ingredients:

½ c. raisins
1 Tbs. brandy (or brandy flavoring)
2 pkg. cream cheese, softened (8 oz. ea.)
½ c. whipping cream
½ tsp. vanilla extract
¼ c. dark brown sugar
1 tsp. cinnamon
½ c. miniature chocolate chips
    cinnamon, for garnish

Directions:

1. In small bowl, mix raisins and brandy together. Soak 15 minutes.
2. In another bowl, beat cream cheese and whipping cream until smooth.
3. Add vanilla; mix well.
4. Blend in brown sugar and cinnamon.
5. Mix in soaked raisins and chocolate chips, blending well.
6. Garnish with a light dusting of cinnamon.
7. Serve at room temperature with assorted plain cookies and sweet crackers.

Did You Know? . . . .

Did you know that by pouring leftover chocolate onto a piece of wax paper makes for easier clean up. Let the chocolate cool so that you can break and re-melt it later.

Strawberry and Chocolate Tortilla

If you need a quick, sweet treat, this is easy to make and satisfying. If you roll the tortillas up tightly, you can slice each burrito-style tortilla in 1-inch slices and serve them as an appetizer.

Ingredients:

   2 sm. flour tortillas
   4 Tbs. Belgian chocolate, chopped
   1 c. fresh strawberries, sliced
      powdered sugar

Directions:

   1. Sprinkle each tortilla with 2 tablespoons chopped chocolate.
   2. Place on paper towel in microwave.
   3. Heat on high for 30 seconds.
   4. Place the strawberries in center of tortilla and roll up.
   5. To serve, place on individual plates with edge down.
   6. Sprinkle lightly with powdered sugar.

Crock Pot Trail Mix

This is very simple to make and is a delicious appetizer.

Ingredients:

   4 c. rolled oats
   ⅔ c. honey
   1 c. bran flakes
   ¼ c. canola oil
   1 c. wheat germ
   1 tsp. cinnamon
   2 Tbs. cocoa
   ½ c. sesame seeds

Directions:

   1. Combine all ingredients in a slow cooker.

2. Cook on low heat with lid slightly ajar about 4 hours, stirring occasionally.
3. Cool and store in airtight jar.
4. Use within 1 to 2 weeks.

Chocolate Caramel Popcorn

Everybody loves caramel popcorn, and this recipe is delicious.

Ingredients:

14 oz. caramels
3 Tbs. butter
2 Tbs. water
12 c. air-popped popcorn (2 c. unpopped)
1 c. peanuts or other nut of choice
1 c. chocolate chips, melted

Directions

1. Preheat oven to 300 degrees F.
2. Microwave caramels, butter, and water in a microwave-safe bowl on high for 2 to 3 minutes, or until caramels are completely melted.
3. Stir after each minute of heating.
4. Combine popcorn and peanuts in a large bowl.
5. Drizzle caramel mixture over the popcorn and peanuts; mix to coat.
6. Spread popcorn out on a greased baking sheet.
7. Bake for 20 minutes, stirring after 10 minutes.
8. Melt chocolate chips; spread over baked popcorn mixture and stir to combine.
9. Spread popcorn out on wax paper to cool.
10. You may need to break some of the pieces into smaller clusters.
11. Store in a covered container at room temperature for up to one week.

Yields: 18 servings.

Chocolate-Sesame Dipped Strawberries

Toasted sesame seeds add extra crunch and a tasty surprise to this easy-to-eat dessert. Look for large strawberries with stems for the nicest presentation.

Ingredients:

⅓ c. walnut pieces, finely chopped
2 Tbs. sesame seeds
3 oz. bittersweet chocolate
2 Tbs. half and half cream
20 lg. strawberries with stems, rinsed, dried

Directions:

1. Preheat oven to 275 degrees F.
2. Spread walnuts on a baking sheet.
3. Bake 10 minutes until fragrant and lightly browned.
4. While nuts are toasting, place sesame seeds in a small skillet over medium-low heat.
5. Cook, gently shaking pan back and forth, until seeds are golden, about 5 minutes.
6. Allow nuts and seeds to cool; mix together in a shallow bowl.
7. In small saucepan, over medium-low heat, add chocolate and cream.
8. Whisk together for 3 minutes, or until chocolate is melted.
9. Line a baking pan with wax paper.
10. Dip strawberries into chocolate about ¾ of the way in.
11. Dip one side into nut and seed mixture, coating well.
12. Place nut side up in baking pan.
13. Refrigerate 15 minutes, or until chocolate is set.
14. Serve.

Chocolate Delights
A Collection of Chocolate Recipes
Cookbook Delights Series Book 3

Beverages

Table of Contents

Page

Almond Cocoa

The almond extract enhances the flavor of hot cocoa. Try this warm drink the next time you are feeling chilly.

Ingredients:

    2 Tbs. sugar
    2 Tbs. cocoa powder, unsweetened
    3 c. milk
    ½ tsp. vanilla extract
    10 drops almond extract

Directions:

1. In medium saucepan, combine sugar and cocoa powder.
2. Gradually stir in milk until smooth.
3. Heat over medium heat until warm.
4. Remove from heat.
5. Stir in vanilla and almond extract.

Yields: 4 servings.

Amaretto Fudge Cappuccino

This is a delicious hot beverage, and you may add more of any of the flavorings if you prefer your cappuccino with a stronger chocolate or amaretto flavor.

Ingredients:

    1 c. water, boiling
    1 Tbs. instant coffee
    1 Tbs. amaretto syrup
    1 Tbs. chocolate syrup
    2 Tbs. cream
       sweetened whipped cream, for garnish
       chocolate shavings, for garnish

Directions:

1. Combine water and instant coffee in large mug; stir until coffee is dissolved.
2. Stir in cream, amaretto syrup, and chocolate syrup.
3. Top with sweetened whipped cream and chocolate shavings, if desired.

Yields: 1 serving.

Blueberry Chocolate Cream Coffee

Serve this drink on a nippy early morning. It will warm you up deliciously.

Ingredients:

8 Tbs. blueberry syrup
4 Tbs. chocolate syrup
1 c. heavy cream, reserve 4 Tbs.
3 c. hot coffee
4 sprinkles ground cinnamon
4 pinches grated orange peel
   sweetened whipped cream

Directions:

1. Whip together syrups and cream; reserve 4 tablespoons of cream.
2. Stir reserved cream and blueberry syrup in saucepan over low heat until mixed together.
3. Add coffee gradually while stirring mixture.
4. Pour evenly into 4 warmed mugs.
5. Top with whipped cream, a sprinkle of cinnamon, and a pinch of grated orange peel.

Yields: 4 servings.

Cafe Mexicano

This is a wonderful cup of coffee for first thing in the morning. You will want one the next morning, and the next.

Ingredients:

4   tsp. chocolate syrup
½   c. heavy cream
¾   tsp. cinnamon, divided
¼   tsp. nutmeg
1   Tbs. sugar
1½ c. strong hot coffee

Directions:

1. Pour 1 teaspoon chocolate syrup in each of 4 coffee cups.
2. In large mixing bowl, combine heavy cream, ¼ teaspoon cinnamon, nutmeg, and sugar.
3. Whip until soft peaks form.
4. Stir remaining cinnamon into hot coffee.
5. Divide the coffee evenly between the 4 mugs, and stir each to blend the coffee with chocolate syrup.
6. Top each cup with the spiced whipped cream mixture and serve immediately.

Yields: 4 servings.

Peppermint Cocoa

This is a fun and creamy hot chocolate with peppermint to serve to peppermint lovers year round.

Ingredients:

4   c. milk
3   sq. semi-sweet chocolate, chopped (1 oz. ea.)

¼ c. peppermint candy, crushed
1 c. whipped cream

Directions:

1. In medium saucepan, heat milk until hot, but not boiling.
2. Whisk in chocolate and peppermint candies until melted and smooth.
3. Pour hot cocoa into 4 mugs and garnish with whipped cream.

Chocolate-Banana-Peanut Butter Malt

This makes a nutritious as well as delicious breakfast drink for those who need to eat on the run.

Ingredients:

1 c. milk
½ c. ice cubes
1 Tbs. creamy peanut butter
2 Tbs. chocolate malt powder
1 banana

Directions:

1. Place milk, malt powder, banana, and peanut butter in blender.
2. Cover and blend until smooth.
3. Add ice, blend until smooth.
4. Pour into glass and serve immediately.

Did You Know? . . . .

Did you know that the lighter in color the chocolate, the more easily it burns?

Chocoberry Milk Chiller

Chocolate and blueberries blend to form a rich and delightful drink.

Ingredients:

> 1 c. chocolate milk
> 4 Tbs. chocolate syrup, divided
> 2 Tbs. blueberry syrup (see recipe on page 190)
>   multicolored sprinkles, if desired
>   fresh or frozen blueberries, if desired

Directions:

1. In medium bowl, stir 2 tablespoons chocolate syrup and 2 tablespoons blueberry syrup into chocolate milk, and mix thoroughly.
2. Chill mixture in freezer for 5 minutes.
3. While mixture is chilling, dip rims of 2 chilled glasses upside down into remaining chocolate syrup and then sprinkles, to coat edges, if desired.
4. Drizzle remaining chocolate syrup on inside and bottom of glasses.
5. Pull mixture out of freezer; pour into chocolate drizzled glasses.
6. Garnish with blueberries, if desired.

Yields: 2 servings.

Chocolate Eggnog

Try this recipe for a change of pace to the regular drink. Adults and children alike enjoy it.

Ingredients:

> 4 c. chocolate milk

3 c. prepared eggnog (dairy-pasteurized)
1 sprinkle ground nutmeg

Directions:

1. Combine chocolate milk and eggnog in large
   pitcher or bowl; refrigerate.
2. Pour into glasses.
3. Sprinkle with nutmeg.

Yields: 6 servings.

Coffee Mocha Punch

This is truly a delicious coffee-lover's punch.

Ingredients:

1 qt. coffee, extra-strength, chilled breakfast blend
1 qt. chocolate ice cream
1 qt. vanilla ice cream
1 c. whipping cream
¼ tsp. salt
½ c. sugar
¼ tsp. almond extract
½ tsp. vanilla extract
½ tsp. nutmeg
¼ tsp. cinnamon (optional)

Directions:

1. Pour chilled coffee into punch bowl.
2. Add walnut-size chunks of ice cream.
3. Whip cream, adding salt, sugar, almond extract, and
   vanilla; fold into punch.
4. Sprinkle with nutmeg and cinnamon.

Yields: 35 servings.

Chocolate Malted Milk Shake

Our family loves chocolate malts. Be sure and taste both the vanilla malts and the chocolate malts to see which you enjoy more.

Ingredients:

>   1 pt. chocolate ice cream
>   ¼ c. whole milk
>   1 Tbs. malt (more for stronger malt flavor)
>   2 Tbs. chocolate syrup

Directions:

1. Place all ingredients in a blender.
2. Process on low speed until all ingredients are well incorporated and a smooth shake forms, usually 30 to 45 seconds.

Yields: 2 servings.

Chocolate Peanut Butter Shake

If you like a richer chocolate flavor, just add chocolate syrup to your taste preference. This is reminiscent of a frozen peanut butter cup in flavor.

Ingredients:

>   1 c. milk
>   2 c. chocolate ice cream or frozen yogurt
>   ⅓ c. ice cubes
>   3 Tbs. creamy peanut butter

Directions:

1. Place milk, ice cream, ice, and peanut butter in blender.
2. Cover and blend until smooth.

Yields: 2 servings.

Frothy Cappuccino Punch

This is a great punch for all those coffee-lovers.

Ingredients:

1 gal. freshly brewed coffee, double-strength, chilled (measure 2 rounded Tbs. ground coffee to every 6 oz. water)
3 cans evaporated milk (12 oz. ea.), chilled, divided
1 c. sugar, divided
1 tsp. vanilla extract
1 qt. chocolate ice cream
semi-sweet chocolate baking bars, made into curls
ground cinnamon

Directions:

1. Pour coffee into large punch bowl.
2. Combine 2¼ cups evaporated milk, ½ cup sugar, and vanilla extract in blender; blend until frothy.
3. Add milk mixture to coffee.
4. Repeat with remaining evaporated milk and remaining sugar.
5. Add scoops of ice cream to punch; top with chocolate curls.
6. Ladle punch into cups; sprinkle with cinnamon.
7. Hint: To make chocolate curls, carefully draw vegetable peeler across bar of chocolate. Vary width of curls by using different sides of chocolate bar.

Yields: 50 servings.

Chocolate Strawberry Frost

Frost your glass by putting it in the freezer at least an hour before using, or overnight is even better. Be sure to use a thick glass.

Ingredients:

> 1 c. vanilla frozen yogurt or ice cream
> 1 c. frozen or fresh strawberries
> ½ c. milk
> 2 Tbs. chocolate syrup

Directions:

> 1. Place frozen yogurt or ice cream, strawberries, milk, and chocolate syrup in blender.
> 2. Cover and blend until smooth.
> 3. Pour into a large, heavy glass that has been in freezer overnight.

Yields: 1 serving.

Chocolate Raspberry Yogurt Smoothie

This is a great breakfast on the go or snack when you are in a hurry.

Ingredients:

> ½ c. milk
> 1 c. yogurt (plain, vanilla or raspberry)
> 2 Tbs. chocolate syrup
> ½ c. fresh or frozen raspberries

Directions:

1. Place milk, yogurt, chocolate syrup, and raspberries in blender.
2. Cover and blend until smooth.

Yields: 1 large serving.

Cinnamon Chocolate Coffee

This is a flavorful blend of chocolate, orange, coffee, and cinnamon that I am sure you will enjoy.

Ingredients:

4¼ c. water
½ c. ground coffee
4 whole cloves
1 cinnamon stick
½ c. milk
¼ lb. dark chocolate, chopped
2 tsp. orange zest

Directions:

1. Combine coffee, cloves, and cinnamon.
2. Brew according to desired method.
3. Heat milk and chocolate in heavy saucepan over low heat.
4. Stir until mixture is smooth.
5. Stir in hot coffee, a little at a time, whisking until mixture is frothy.
6. Serve coffee sprinkled with orange zest.
7. Sweeten to taste.

Yields: 4 servings.

Spiced Hot Chocolate

Try this delectable combination of cinnamon, orange, and chocolate. It is delicious.

Ingredients:

    32 oz. semi-sweet chocolate, broken in pieces
    2   Tbs. orange peel, finely grated
    3   tsp. ground cinnamon
    15 c. milk
    2½ c. sweetened whipping cream
    15 cinnamon sticks (3 inches ea.)
        chocolate, grated

Directions:

1. Combine chocolate, orange peel, cinnamon, and 3 tablespoons milk in a saucepan.
2. Heat very gently until chocolate melts, stirring frequently.
3. Add remaining milk and heat through gently until piping hot, stirring frequently.
4. Whisk whipping cream until soft peaks form.
5. Pour hot chocolate into mugs or heatproof glasses.
6. Top with whipped cream.
7. Sprinkle with grated chocolate.
8. Add a cinnamon stick to each one for stirring.

Yields: 15 servings.

White Hot Chocolate

This white hot chocolate is a fun change of pace from the usual hot chocolate.

Ingredients:

    6   oz. white chocolate, divided
    ½   c. heavy cream

1 qt. milk
¼ c. amaretto or, for children, ½ tsp. almond extract

Directions:

1. Coarsely grate ½ ounce white chocolate for garnish; set aside.
2. In small mixing bowl, beat heavy cream until stiff peaks form; set aside.
3. Chop remaining chocolate into chunks.
4. In medium saucepan over medium heat, heat chocolate and milk, stirring constantly until chocolate is completely melted.
5. Remove from heat; stir in amaretto or almond extract.
6. Pour into 5 mugs; top with dollop of whipped cream, and garnish with reserved white chocolate.

Yields: 5 servings.

Cocoa Espresso Cooler

This is a refreshing iced coffee to enjoy on those warm summer days. You may substitute very strong instant coffee for the espresso if you don't have an espresso machine.

Ingredients:

2 c. espresso blend coffee, cold
2 c. prepared cocoa, cold
1 tsp. vanilla extract
4 Tbs. sweetened whipped cream

Directions:

1. Combine cold coffee, cocoa, and vanilla.
2. Pour over ice in tall glasses.
3. Top each with 2 tablespoons whipped cream.

Yields: 2 servings.

Crockpot Hot Mint Malt

This is rich and creamy for chocolate mint lovers.

Ingredients:

    6   chocolate-covered peppermint patties
    5   c. milk
    ½ c. chocolate malted milk powder
    1   tsp. vanilla extract
        whipped cream

Directions:

1. In slow-cooking pot, combine mint patties with milk, malted milk powder, and vanilla.
2. Heat on low for 2 hours then beat until frothy.
3. Pour into cups; top with sweetened whipped cream.

Mexican Coffee

This is a delicious and rich coffee with cinnamon.

Ingredients:

    ¾ c. Mexican Altura coffee beans, ground
    2   tsp. ground cinnamon
    6   c. water
    1   c. milk
    ½ c. chocolate syrup
    2   Tbs. light brown sugar
    1   tsp. pure vanilla extract
        whipped cream, for garnish

Directions:

1. Place coffee and cinnamon in basket of coffee maker.
2. Add water to coffee maker and brew as directed.
3. In saucepan, blend milk, chocolate syrup, and sugar.
4. Stir over low heat until sugar dissolves; then combine with brewed coffee and stir in vanilla.
5. Garnish with whipped cream and cinnamon.

Chocolate Delights
A Collection of Chocolate Recipes
Cookbook Delights Series Book 3

Breads and Rolls

Table of Contents

Page

Choco Chip Pumpkin Muffins

This combination of chocolate chips and pumpkin is just wonderful with breakfast for a large holiday gathering.

Ingredients:

- 2   c. brown sugar
- 1   can pure pumpkin purée (15 oz.)
- 1   c. light tasting olive oil
- ⅔   c. water
- 4   lg. eggs
- 3⅓ c. flour
- 1   Tbs. ground cinnamon
- 1   tsp. ground nutmeg
- 1   tsp. ginger
- ¼   tsp. allspice
- ⅛   tsp. cloves
- 2   tsp. baking soda
- 1½ tsp. salt
- 1½ c. semi-sweet miniature chocolate chips

Directions:

1. Preheat oven to 350 degrees F.
2. Line muffin tins with papers.
3. In large bowl, blend pumpkin, oil, water, and eggs until smooth.
4. In another bowl, combine all dry ingredients together; gradually blend into pumpkin mixture.
5. Fold in chocolate chips (do not use mixer).
6. Fill muffin tins ¾ full.
7. Bake 15 to 19 minutes, or until an inserted toothpick comes out clean.
8. Cool on wire racks before removing from tins.

Yields: 36 servings.

Chocolate Sour Cream Muffins

These chocolate muffins are delicious with sour cream.

Ingredients:

5 oz. semi-sweet chocolate
2 baking chocolate squares
⅓ c. butter
¾ c. sour cream
⅔ c. brown sugar, packed
¼ c. corn syrup
1 egg
2 tsp. vanilla extract
1½ c. flour
1 tsp. baking soda
¼ tsp. salt
½ c. chocolate chips

Directions:

1. Preheat oven to 400 degrees F.
2. Paper-line 12 muffin cups.
3. In top of double boiler or microwaveable bowl, combine semi-sweet chocolate, baking chocolate, and butter together.
4. Melt over simmering water in double boiler or in microwave.
5. Cool to lukewarm.
6. In medium bowl, combine sour cream, sugar, corn syrup, egg, and vanilla.
7. Blend with melted chocolates.
8. In large bowl, blend flour, baking soda, and salt.
9. Add chocolate mixture and blend well.
10. Stir in chocolate chips.
11. Pour batter into prepared muffins cups.
12. Bake 20 minutes.
13. Remove from muffin tins; cool.

Chocolate Apple Bread

It is the chocolate that makes this bread special for both adults and children.

Ingredients for topping:

    2   Tbs. sugar
    ¼   tsp. ground cinnamon
    ½   c. walnuts, finely chopped

Ingredients for bread:

    2   c. flour
    ½   tsp. salt
    ½   tsp. baking powder
    ½   tsp. baking soda
    ¾   tsp. ground cinnamon
    ¼   tsp. ground nutmeg
    ½   c. butter, softened
    1   c. sugar
    2   eggs
    1   tsp. vanilla extract
    2   Tbs. buttermilk
    1¼ c. apples, chopped
    1   c. walnuts, finely chopped
    ¾   c. semi-sweet chocolate chips

Directions for topping:

1. In small bowl, combine sugar, cinnamon, and walnuts; set aside.

Directions for bread:

1. Preheat oven to 350 degrees F.
2. Lightly grease a 9 x 5 x 3-inch loaf pan.
3. In medium bowl, combine flour, salt, baking powder, baking soda, cinnamon, and nutmeg; set aside.
4. In a separate large bowl, cream butter and sugar.
5. Add eggs and vanilla to creamed mixture; mix well.

6. Gradually beat in flour mixture alternately with buttermilk.
7. Stir in apples, walnuts, and chocolate chips.
8. Pour into prepared pan; sprinkle with topping.
9. Bake 50 to 60 minutes.
10. Cool 15 minutes, then remove from pan.
11. Cool on wire rack.
12. Cut or slice after completely cooled.

Raspberry Chip Bread

Raspberries make this bread taste like a bit of summer all year round. Don't be afraid to double the recipe, as it also freezes well.

Ingredients:

3   c. flour
2   c. sugar
3   tsp. cinnamon
1   tsp. baking soda
1   tsp. salt
20 oz. frozen raspberries, thawed, drained
4   eggs, beaten
1¼ c. canola oil
1   c. walnuts or pecans, chopped
1   c. semi-sweet chocolate chips

Directions:

1. Preheat oven to 350 degrees F.
2. Well grease two loaf pans.
3. Mix flour, sugar, cinnamon, baking soda, and salt together.
4. Mash raspberries well; add eggs and oil.
5. Combine raspberry mixture with flour mixture; add chocolate chips. Mix well.
6. Pour into prepared pans.
7. Bake 1 hour, or until inserted toothpick in center comes out clean.

Chocolate Banana Bread

This is a moist bread with the delicious flavor of chocolate for those that just can't get enough of that delectable treat.

Ingredients:

> 2 c. flour
> ¾ c. sugar, divided
> ½ c. cocoa
> ¾ tsp. baking soda
> ½ tsp. baking powder
> ¼ tsp. salt
> 1 c. plain yogurt (8 oz.)
> ½ c. ripe banana, mashed
> ⅓ c. canola oil
> ⅓ c. milk
> 2 tsp. vanilla extract
> 3 egg whites

Directions:

1. Preheat oven to 350 degrees F.
2. Lightly grease and flour a loaf pan.
3. In large bowl, combine flour, ¼ cup sugar, cocoa, baking soda, baking powder, and salt; set aside.
4. In medium bowl, stir together yogurt, banana, milk, oil, and vanilla; set aside.
5. In small bowl, beat egg whites until foamy.
6. Gradually add remaining ½ cup sugar, beating well after each addition until stiff peaks form.
7. Stir yogurt mixture into flour mixture until moistened; fold in ⅓ of egg white mixture.
8. Gently fold in remaining egg white mixture.
9. Fill prepared loaf pan ⅔ full with batter.
10. Bake 35 to 45 minutes, or until inserted toothpick in center comes out clean.

11. Remove from pan to wire rack.
12. Cool completely before slicing.

Yields: 1 loaf.

Chocolate Tea Bread

Serve this fresh-made chocolate bread with your favorite tea.

Ingredients:

¼ c. butter, softened
⅔ c. sugar
1 egg
1½ c. flour
⅓ c. baking cocoa
1 tsp. baking soda
¼ tsp. salt
1 c. buttermilk

Directions:

1. Preheat oven to 350 degrees F.
2. Lightly grease an 8½ x 4½ x 2½-inch loaf pan.
3. In large bowl, cream butter, sugar, and egg until light and fluffy.
4. Combine flour, cocoa, baking soda, and salt.
5. Add alternately with buttermilk to creamed mixture.
6. With electric mixer on low speed, beat just until blended.
7. Pour into prepared pan.
8. Bake for 55 to 60 minutes.
9. Remove from pan; cool completely on wire rack, and slice.

Yields: 8 to 10 servings.

Chocolate Brownie Bread

This is delicious bread for a snack and also a great lunchbox treat.

Ingredients:

4 sq. unsweetened baking chocolate
½ c. butter
1 c. sugar
1 c. brown sugar, firmly packed
2 eggs
1 c. sour cream
1 tsp. vanilla extract
1½ c. flour
2 tsp. baking powder
¼ tsp. baking soda
1 c. walnuts, toasted, finely chopped

Directions:

1. Preheat oven to 350 degrees F.
2. Grease and flour a 9 x 5-inch loaf pan.
3. In small saucepan, over medium heat, melt chocolate and butter, stirring until completely melted.
4. Add sugars; mix well.
5. Blend in eggs, sour cream, and vanilla.
6. Add flour, baking powder, and baking soda; mix well.
7. Stir in walnuts.
8. Spread into prepared pan.
9. Bake 60 to 70 minutes, or until inserted toothpick in center comes out clean.
10. Cool in pan 10 minutes.
11. Remove from pan to wire rack.
12. Slice when completely cooled.

Chocolate Chip Muffins

Chocolate chip muffins are always a special treat.

Ingredients:

 2 c. flour
 ⅓ c. brown sugar
 ⅓ c. sugar
 2 tsp. baking powder
 ½ tsp. salt
 ⅔ c. milk
 ½ c. butter, melted, cooled
 2 eggs, beaten
 1 tsp. vanilla extract
 1 pkg. chocolate chips (12 oz.)
 ½ c. walnuts or pecans, chopped

Directions:

1. Preheat oven to 400 degrees F.
2. Lightly grease or paper-line 12 muffin cups.
3. In large bowl, stir together flour, sugars, baking powder, and salt.
4. In another bowl, stir together milk, eggs, butter, and vanilla until blended.
5. Make a well in center of dry ingredients.
6. Add milk mixture and stir just to combine.
7. Stir in chocolate chips and nuts.
8. Spoon batter into muffin cups.
9. Bake 15 to 20 minutes, or until a knife inserted in center of one muffin comes out clean.
10. Remove muffin tin to wire rack; cool 5 minutes.
11. Remove from tins to finish cooling.
12. Serve warm.

Yields: 12 servings.

Chocolate Doughnuts

You cannot buy a doughnut that even comes close to homemade doughnuts. You will love these.

Ingredients for doughnuts:

1	qt. canola oil (or enough to fill frying pot 3 inches deep)
½	c. dark brown sugar, packed
2	Tbs. butter
2	c. flour plus 3 Tbs. for work surface and 3-inch doughnut cutter
½	tsp. salt
2½	tsp. baking powder
½	tsp. baking soda
2	Tbs. Callebaut unsweetened cocoa (if other cocoa, double amount)
1	egg
1	tsp. pure vanilla extract
½	c. sour cream

Ingredients for chocolate icing:

¾	c. powdered sugar
2	Tbs. Callebaut cocoa
½	tsp. lemon juice
1	egg white
2	tsp. water

Directions for doughnuts:

1. Preheat oil in a heavy pot to 320 degrees F. Use a thermometer.
2. Beat brown sugar and butter together, using standing mixer and paddle attachment, until creamed.
3. In large bowl, sift together 2 cups flour, salt, baking powder, baking soda, and cocoa; set aside.
4. Beat egg and vanilla together; add to the mixer, beating to combine.

5. In the adding, beating, stopping, scraping-down sequence, add ⅓ of the flour mixture to the mixer, then ½ the sour cream, ⅓ flour, half the sour cream, and ⅓ flour. Do not over beat.
6. Bring the dough together onto your work surface.
7. Flour work surface if dough is sticky; roll out to ½-inch thickness.
8. Using doughnut cutter, cut out doughnuts from the edge. Flour the cutter if the dough sticks to it.
9. Save the holes for cooking, too.
10. If kitchen is warm, place doughnuts on a lightly floured baking sheet and put in the refrigerator for 15 to 20 minutes. Cooler dough is easier to handle.
11. Check temperature of the oil, and bring it up to 375 degrees F. Try to ease it up there; if the oil gets too hot it will start to smoke. You can also check to see if the oil's hot enough by dropping in a chunk of bread. It should immediately bob to the surface, lightly browned.
12. Put doughnuts in hot oil 2 or 3 at a time, depending on size of pot. They should be able to move around in the oil.
13. Cook 3 to 4 minutes on the first side, turn, and cook another 2 to 3 minutes on the second side.
14. Make sure your wire spoon is dry. No water should ever come in contact with the hot oil as severe burns from spattering could result.
15. As the doughnuts are finished, transfer them to a paper towel.
16. Cool 10 minutes before icing.

Directions for chocolate icing:

1. Sift powdered sugar and cocoa together into a bowl.
2. Add remaining ingredients; whisk together until smooth.
3. Spread icing on cooled doughnuts.

Yields: 8 servings.

Chocolate Chip Pumpkin Bread

This bread is moist and freezes well. The chocolate and nuts are a great combination with the pumpkin. Try baking the loaves in coffee cans and wrapping in colored cellophane to give as gifts.

Ingredients:

    3   c. sugar
    1   can pumpkin purée (15 oz.)
    1   c. canola oil
    ⅔ c. water
    4   eggs
    3½ c. flour
    1   Tbs. ground cinnamon
    1   Tbs. ground nutmeg
    2   tsp. baking soda
    1½ tsp. salt
    1¼ c. semi-sweet chocolate chips, miniature
    1¼ c. walnuts, chopped

Directions:

1. Preheat oven to 350 degrees F.
2. Grease and flour three 1-pound coffee cans or three 9 x 5-inch loaf pans.
3. In large bowl, combine sugar, pumpkin, oil, water, and eggs; beat until smooth.
4. In medium bowl, combine flour, cinnamon, nutmeg, baking soda, and salt.
5. Stir into sugar mixture; mix well.
6. Fold in chocolate chips and nuts.
7. Fill cans ½ to ¾ full.
8. Bake 1 hour, or until knife inserted in center comes out clean.
9. Cool on wire racks before removing from cans or pans.

Yields: 3 loaves.

Cranberry Choconut Bread

This is a colorful, moist bread that is great for the holidays.

Ingredients:

2¼ c. flour
¾ c. sugar
1½ tsp. baking powder
¾ tsp. baking soda
¾ tsp. salt
⅓ c. butter, softened
1 Tbs. orange peel, grated
⅓ c. orange juice
2 eggs
1¼ c. fresh or frozen cranberries, chopped
1½ c. nuts, chopped
1 c. chocolate chips, miniature

Directions:

1. Preheat oven to 350 degrees F.
2. Lightly grease and flour a loaf pan.
3. In large bowl, combine flour, sugar, baking powder, salt, and baking soda.
4. Stir in butter until mixture is crumbly.
5. Stir in orange peel, orange juice, and eggs just until all flour is moistened.
6. Stir in cranberries, nuts, and chocolate chips.
7. Pour into prepared pan.
8. Bake 55 to 65 minutes, or until inserted toothpick in center comes out clean.
9. Loosen sides of loaf from pan, remove from pan.
10. Cool completely on wire rack before slicing.

Did You Know? . . . .

Did you know that the presence of theobromine renders chocolate toxic to some animals?

Chocolate Orange Honey Buns

These are melt-in-your-mouth delicious, and are wonderful served for a late breakfast or brunch on the weekend. Serve them warm from the oven.

Ingredients for buns:

    1   pkg. active dry yeast
    1   c. milk, warm
    2   Tbs. sugar
    2   Tbs. honey
    1   tsp. salt
    2   lg. eggs, lightly beaten
    2   tsp. orange rind, grated
    ½ c. butter, melted
    4¼ c. flour
    2   Tbs. butter, melted

Ingredients for orange sugar filling:

    ½ c. sugar
    4   tsp. orange rind, grated
    ¼ c. almonds, finely sliced

Ingredients for honey topping:

    4   Tbs. butter
    ½ c. honey
    ⅓ c. sugar

Directions:

1. In large bowl, add warm milk, then sprinkle yeast over milk and stir until yeast dissolves.
2. Add sugar, honey, salt, eggs, orange rind, and half the butter and flour; beat well.

3. Mix in remaining butter and enough flour to form soft dough.
4. Knead, cover, and let rise 1 hour, until double in bulk.
5. Mix orange filling ingredients and set aside.
6. Divide dough in half and roll out into 8 x 12-inch rectangles.
7. Brush both dough rectangles with melted butter and sprinkle the orange sugar filling over top.
8. Roll up from long edge and slice into 1-inch pieces.
9. In small saucepan, combine honey topping ingredients; bring to rapid boil.
10. Pour into a 9 x 13-inch baking pan.
11. Place sliced buns into the pan with the honey topping, cover, and let rise 30 minutes until double in size.
12. Preheat oven to 375 degrees F.
13. Bake 25 minutes, or until golden.
14. Remove from oven; immediately turn the pan upside down onto foil.
15. The buns are best when eaten warm or at room temperature.

Did You Know? . . . .

Did you know that experts now believe one sweet treat is actually smart for your heart? Dark chocolate, ounce for ounce, contains more antioxidants than even the highest-antioxidant fruits and vegetables. The antioxidants it contains, called flavonols, perform miracles on your blood vessels, guarding against the buildup of sticky plaque on artery walls and also keeping arteries elastic. The end result: a lower risk of heart disease, the number one killer of people with diabetes.

Stick with 1 ounce a day, and make sure it's dark chocolate, as milk chocolate doesn't offer the same benefits and can raise cholesterol. Choose a dark chocolate with the highest cocoa content you can find. Or bake with pure cocoa powder, which contains even more antioxidants than a dark chocolate bar.

Chocolate Zucchini Bread

For some reason, zucchini puts its best foot forward when combined with chocolate. This is delicious!

Ingredients:

- 3   eggs
- ¾ c. canola oil
- 2   tsp. vanilla extract
- 2⅓ c. flour
- ½ tsp. baking powder
- 2   tsp. baking soda
- ½ c. unsweetened cocoa
- 1   tsp. cinnamon
- 1   tsp. salt
- 1½ c. sugar
- 3   c. zucchini, grated
- ½ c. nuts (optional)

Directions:

1. Preheat oven to 350 degrees F.
2. Lightly grease two loaf pans.
3. In large bowl, combine eggs, oil, and vanilla.
4. Set aside.
5. In medium bowl, combine flour, baking powder, baking soda, cocoa, cinnamon, salt, and sugar.
6. Combine flour mixture with egg mixture.
7. Stir in zucchini and nuts.
8. Pour into prepared pans.
9. Bake 45 minutes, or until inserted toothpick in center comes out clean.
10. Cool on wire racks.

Did You Know? . . . .

Did you know there are 40 to 50 million people worldwide who depend upon cocoa for their livelihood?

Heavenly Chocolate Bread

This delicious chocolate bread is sweet, but not too sweet, and moist.

Ingredients:

4 oz. unsweetened chocolate or 12 Tbs. cocoa powder
½ c. butter
4 eggs
⅔ c. honey
2 c. potatoes, mashed
½ c. brandy, rum, orange juice, or a mixture
2 tsp. vanilla extract
2 tsp. orange zest
2¼ c. flour
4 tsp. baking powder
1 tsp. salt

Directions:

1. Preheat oven to 350 degrees F.
2. Lightly grease three 7 x 3-inch loaf pans.
3. In a microwaveable bowl, melt chocolate and butter; mix together.
4. In another bowl, beat eggs until frothy.
5. Add honey, mashed potatoes, alcohol, and/or juice, vanilla, and orange zest.
6. Stir in chocolate-butter mixture.
7. In separate bowl, mix together flour, baking powder, and salt.
8. Stir 2 cups of flour mixture into wet mixture. The mixture should be a heavy batter.
9. If too thin, add rest of the flour mixture and stir until everything is moistened.
10. Pour batter into prepared pans.
11. Bake on center rack, 40 minutes, or until inserted toothpick comes out clean.

Strawberry Chocolate Chip Bread

This bread is absolutely delicious, and the children especially like the chocolate chips.

Ingredients:

½ c. butter
1½ c. sugar
1 tsp. vanilla extract
1 tsp. salt
1 tsp. lemon juice
4 eggs
½ tsp. baking soda
½ c. sour cream
3 c. flour
½ c. chocolate chips
1 c. strawberry preserves
1 Tbs. red food coloring

Directions:

1. Preheat oven to 350 degrees F.
2. Lightly grease and flour two loaf pans.
3. In large bowl, blend butter, sugar, vanilla, salt, and juice.
4. Beat in eggs one at a time.
5. Dissolve baking soda in sour cream; add to egg mixture.
6. Blend in the flour and fold in chocolate chips, strawberry preserves, and coloring.
7. Pour into prepared pans.
8. Bake 35 to 40 minutes, or until inserted toothpick comes out clean.
9. Remove from oven.
10. Cool 10 minutes.
11. Turn out onto wire rack to cool completely.

Chocolate Delights
A Collection of Chocolate Recipes
Cookbook Delights Series Book 3

Breakfasts

Table of Contents

Page

Chocolate Bread with Raspberry Syrup

These are a dream come true for breakfast.

Ingredients for raspberry syrup:

> 2½ c. frozen raspberries, thawed, with juice
> 1   c. sugar
> 1   c. light corn syrup

Ingredients for bread:

> 2½ c. flour
> 1½ tsp. baking soda
> ½ c. cocoa
> 1   c. sugar
> ½ tsp. salt
> 1   egg, beaten
> ⅓ c. butter, melted
> 1¼ c. sour milk
> 1   Tbs. vinegar (optional), for souring milk

Directions for raspberry syrup:

1. Place raspberries (including juice) and sugar into a blender and process at high speed.
2. Mash and force through a sieve with potato masher.
3. Pour into saucepan; bring to boil over medium heat.
4. Add corn syrup and cook a little while longer.
5. Pour into serving bottle and set aside.
6. Store leftover syrup in refrigerator.

Directions for bread:

1. Preheat oven to 350 degrees F.
2. Lightly spray a 9 x 5-inch baking pan.
3. In large bowl, sift together flour, baking soda, cocoa, sugar, and salt.
4. If you don't have sour milk, add 1 tablespoon vinegar to 1 cup milk, room temperature.

Allow to sit 5 minutes. I have made this with regular milk and it is good as well.

5. In small bowl, add egg, butter, and sour milk.
6. Combine mixtures until just blended.
7. Fold in ¾ cup chopped walnuts.
8. Pour into prepared loaf pan.
9. Bake 1 hour, or until inserted toothpick in center comes out clean.
10. Slice warm bread and place on small bread plate.
11. Drizzle the raspberry syrup over bread and around plate.
12. Garnish with fresh red raspberries if desired.

Chocolate Breakfast Bars

I always double this recipe and freeze half of them for those busy mornings ahead. They are just wonderful.

Ingredients:

    2   oz. white or dark chocolate
    1½ c. honey
    4   Tbs. butter
    1   Tbs. vanilla extract
    1   c. sunflower seeds or your favorite nut
    ½   c. wheat germ or shredded coconut
    ⅔   c. crunchy peanut butter
    1   c. dried fruit (blueberries, strawberries, or other)
    5   c. quick cooking oats

Directions:

1. In medium saucepan, boil honey, butter, and chocolate for 1 minute.
2. Remove from heat; add vanilla.
3. In medium bowl, combine remaining ingredients; stir into chocolate mixture.
4. Pour dough onto a baking sheet, and flatten it into one large rectangle about 1-inch thick.
5. Let cool, then cut into bars.

Chocolate Caramel French Toast

This will satisfy even the pickiest French toast lover on your list.

Ingredients:

¾ c. brown sugar
¼ c. sugar
½ c. butter
3 Tbs. maple syrup
1½ c. pecans, coarsely chopped
2 c. semi-sweet chocolate chips
20 slices French bread (½-inch slices)
½ c. brown sugar
3 Tbs. butter, melted
6 eggs, beaten
2 tsp. vanilla extract
½ c. heavy cream
1 c. milk
⅓ c. sugar
½ tsp. cinnamon

Directions:

1. In heavy saucepan, combine brown sugar, sugar, butter, and maple syrup; mix until combined.
2. Cook over medium heat until sugar dissolves and mixture is smooth, about 4 to 6 minutes.
3. Pour into a 3-quart 9 x 13-inch baking dish.
4. Sprinkle with half the pecans and half the chocolate chips; top with half the French bread slices.
5. In small bowl combine ½ cup brown sugar and 3 tablespoons melted butter and mix until crumbly.
6. Sprinkle over the French bread slices in pan.
7. Sprinkle with remaining pecans and chocolate chips.
8. Top with remaining French bread slices.

9. In large bowl, combine eggs, vanilla, cream, milk, ⅓ cup sugar, cinnamon, and beat well with eggbeater.
10. Slowly pour this mixture over bread in the baking dish.
11. Press down on bread with spatula to make sure bread absorbs egg mixture.
12. Cover and refrigerate 8 to 24 hours.
13. In the morning, preheat oven to 350 degrees F.
14. Uncover baking dish and bake 35 to 45 minutes until casserole is lightly browned.
15. Let stand for 5 to 10 minutes, then cut into serving-size pieces and invert onto plates.

Yields: 10 servings.

Chocolate Peanut Butter Cup Oatmeal

This recipe has a delicious flavor combination for your breakfast oatmeal.

Ingredients:

1 c. milk
½ c. quick oats
1 Tbs. creamy peanut butter
1 Tbs. semi-sweet chocolate chips
½ tsp. unsweetened cocoa
1 tsp. sugar

Directions:

1. Stirring over medium heat, mix milk and peanut butter together; do not allow to boil.
2. Still stirring, add unsweetened cocoa and sugar.
3. Mix in quick oats, chocolate morsels, and serve while still warm.

Yields: 1 serving.

Chocolate Nut Flapjacks

These pancakes are different from anything you could ever imagine, and they are delicious.

Ingredients:

    1 c. oats
    1 oz. desiccated coconut
    ⅔ c. butter, cut into pieces
    2 oz. light muscovado sugar
    5 Tbs. golden syrup
    4 oz. Brazil nuts or cashews, cut into large chunks
    2 oz. almonds, cut into large chunks
    3 oz. dark chocolate, cut into large chunks

Directions:

1. Preheat oven to 350 degrees F.
2. Lightly butter a 9-inch square baking pan.
3. Line bottom with parchment paper if the pan is not nonstick.
4. In small bowl, combine oats and coconut.
5. In small saucepan, combine butter, sugar, and syrup.
6. Cook over low heat, stirring occasionally, until butter has melted and the sugar is dissolved.
7. Remove from heat; stir in oat mixture.
8. Spoon into prepared pan; press down evenly.
9. Sprinkle nuts over top; press lightly into the mixture.
10. Stick chunks of chocolate between the nuts.
11. Bake 25 to 30 minutes, or until pale golden.
12. Mark the bars or squares with the back of a knife while still warm.
13. Cool completely before cutting through and removing from the pan.

Chocolate Peanut Butter Breakfast Cookies

These are excellent for breakfast, even when you are in a hurry.

Ingredients:

½ c. unsweetened dark cocoa
1½ c. whole wheat flour
1¼ c. rolled oats, quick cooking
¾ c. sugar
1 tsp. cinnamon
1 tsp. salt
2 tsp. baking soda
½ tsp. baking powder
½ c. dark chocolate chips (such as Ghirardelli 60% cacao double chocolate chips)
1 lg. egg
1 tsp. vanilla extract
½ c. applesauce, unsweetened
½ c. natural peanut butter

Directions:

1. Preheat oven to 350 degrees F.
2. In large bowl, whisk together the first 9 ingredients (through the chocolate chips).
3. In small bowl, whisk egg, vanilla, applesauce, and peanut butter together.
4. Pour wet ingredients into the dry and mix well.
5. Line two baking sheets with Silpat mats or parchment paper (optional, but makes cleanup easier).
6. Roll dough into 16 to 20 balls, pressing down to flatten in the shape of a cookie.
7. Place dough on prepared baking sheets 1 inch apart.
8. Bake 8 to 10 minutes.
9. Cool 10 minutes.

Apricot White Chocolate Scones

Apricots and chocolate make a delicious combination in these scones.

Ingredients:

1¾ c. flour
¼ c. sugar
2 tsp. baking powder
¼ tsp. salt
⅓ c. butter, chilled, cut into ¼-inch pieces
⅓ c. dried apricots, finely chopped, divided
⅔ c. white chocolate baking chips, divided
1 egg
⅓ c. half and half cream

Directions:

1. Preheat oven to 400 degrees F.
2. Lightly grease baking sheet with oil, or lightly spray with cooking spray.
3. In large bowl, sift together flour, sugar, baking powder, and salt.
4. With pastry blender, cut butter into flour mixture until particles are pea-size.
5. Reserve 2 tablespoons chopped apricots for topping; set aside.
6. Stir remaining chopped apricots and ⅓ cup white chocolate baking chips into flour mixture.
7. Add egg and just enough cream until dough just leaves side of bowl and forms ball.
8. Note: When making scones, work dough quickly and do not over mix.
9. Place dough on lightly floured surface; knead lightly 10 times.
10. Pat or roll into 8-inch circle on baking sheet.
11. Cut into 8 wedges; do not separate.
12. Bake 15 to 18 minutes, or until golden brown.

13. Remove from oven.
14. Immediately remove from baking sheet; carefully separate wedges.
15. In microwave-safe bowl melt remaining ⅓ cup white chocolate chips in microwave for 20-second intervals.
16. Stir after each interval, even if there is no sign of melting.
17. Once melted, usually after 4 or 5 cycles in the microwave, place melted chocolate chips in small resealable, plastic food-storage bag.
18. Cut off small corner of bag; pipe small amount of melted chips over scones.
19. Sprinkle with reserved 2 tablespoons chopped apricots.
20. Pipe remaining melted chips over scones.
21. Serve warm or cool.
22. Tips: When scones are cool, wrap airtight and hold at room temperature for up to 1 day or freeze to store longer.
23. To reheat, unwrap scones and place on baking sheet.
24. Bake at 350 degrees F. for 8 to 10 minutes, or until warm.
25. If scones are frozen, thaw them while still wrapped, then heat as above.

Yields: 8 scones.

Did You Know? . . . .

Did you know that chocolate contains alkaloids such as theobromine and phenethylamine, which have physiological effects on the body? It has been linked to serotonin levels in the brain. Scientists claim that chocolate, eaten in moderation, can lower blood pressure.

Chocolate Strawberry Waffles

These waffles are actually chocolate waffles, and with the addition of fresh, sweet, summer strawberries in the batter and served over top, they become a mouth watering delight.

Ingredients:

     3   eggs, separated
     ½   c. chocolate syrup
     1½ c. flour
     ¼   c. canola oil
     2   tsp. baking powder
     ¼   c. butter, melted
     ½   tsp. baking soda
     2   c. strawberries, sliced, divided
     2   Tbs. sugar, divided
     1   c. whipping cream
     ½   c. sour cream
     ¾   c. milk

Directions:

1. In small bowl, beat egg whites until stiff; set aside.
2. In large bowl, mix flour, baking powder, baking soda, and 1 tablespoon sugar together.
3. In small bowl, beat egg yolks with sour cream, milk, and chocolate syrup.
4. In another small bowl, mix oil with melted butter.
5. Alternately add sour cream mixture and oil mixture to dry ingredients; mix until smooth.
6. Fold in egg whites and 1 cup of sliced strawberries.
7. Pour ½ cup of batter into a preheated, lightly greased, waffle maker.
8. Cook 4 to 5 minutes or until the steaming stops.
9. Repeat with remainder of batter.
10. In small bowl, whip cream and remaining tablespoon sugar until stiff and fluffy, but not dry.
11. Top with sliced strawberries and whipped cream.

Chocolate Chipotle Waffles

The addition of chipotle pepper powder makes these waffles unique. Try them, you'll be pleasantly surprised.

Ingredients:

2	eggs, lightly beaten
3	Tbs. sugar
¾	c. milk
½	tsp. vanilla extract
½	c. chocolate syrup
4	Tbs. butter, melted
1½	c. cake flour, sifted
3	tsp. baking powder
½	tsp. salt
1½	tsp. chipotle pepper powder, or to taste
	chocolate syrup
	chopped nuts (optional)
	sweetened whipped cream (optional)

Directions:

1. In medium bowl, combine eggs, sugar, milk, and vanilla; stir thoroughly.
2. In another bowl, combine chocolate syrup and butter; cool. Stir into egg mixture.
3. In large bowl, sift flour, baking powder, and salt together.
4. Add egg mixture to dry ingredients; stir until smooth.
5. Stir in chipotle powder, to taste.
6. Lightly grease waffle iron.
7. Heat waffle iron to medium-high.
8. Pour desired amount of batter into waffle iron.
9. Bake until indicator light goes off.
10. Lightly drizzle chocolate syrup over the waffle.
11. Top with whipped cream and nuts, if desired.

Turtle Toast Royale

This is a special treat for those lazy weekend mornings.

Ingredients:

1	lb. loaf French bread
4	oz. cream cheese, room temperature
1	tsp. vanilla extract
2	Tbs. sugar
4	Tbs. pecans, chopped
⅓	c. mini-chocolate chips
4	eggs
1½	c. milk
1	Tbs. sugar

Ingredients for sauce:

½	c. butter
2	c. brown sugar
1	c. whipping cream
1	Tbs. brandy (optional, or use substitute)

Directions:

1. In small bowl, blend cream cheese, vanilla, pecans, and sugar; mix well.
2. Slice end off loaf, then make next slice ½-inch thick, without slicing through to the bottom; then completely slice off the next ½-inch thick piece.
3. Take about 1 tablespoon of the cream cheese mixture and spread it into the pocket formed between the partial cut bread slice.
4. Sprinkle a few chocolate chips into the pocket mixture.
5. In small bowl, combine eggs, milk, and sugar.
6. Dip the stuffed bread into this mixture and turn it over so it becomes evenly coated.

7. Place the toast on an oiled griddle and fry on each side until golden brown.

Directions for sauce:

1. Mix together butter, brown sugar, and whipping cream.
2. Slowly heat over very low heat until it boils.
3. Cook 1 to 2 minutes.
4. Remove from heat and add 1 tablespoon brandy.

Yields: 2 cups.

Chocolate Cookie Oatmeal

You will enjoy this chocolate and peanut butter combination. It tastes just like eating chocolate chip-peanut butter cookies, except with a spoon.

Ingredients:

½   c. instant oatmeal
1   pkg. of instant cocoa
1½ tsp. peanut butter
1   c. water
1   dash of salt
1   tsp. vanilla extract

Directions:

1. Combine all ingredients in a medium saucepan.
2. Cook over medium heat until thick and all ingredients have intermingled (about 3 minutes).

Yields: 1 serving.

Did You Know? . . . .

Did you know that the best things in life are chocolate?

Chocolate Waffles

This makes wonderful chocolate waffles for all to enjoy on those lazy weekend mornings.

Ingredients:

1½ c. flour
3   Tbs. sugar
½   c. cocoa powder
1   tsp. baking powder
1   tsp. salt
½   tsp. baking soda
3   eggs, whole, beaten
¼   c. butter, unsalted, melted, slightly cooled
1   tsp. pure vanilla extract
2   c. buttermilk, room temperature
¾   c. chocolate chips
     canola spray, for waffle iron

Directions:

1. Preheat waffle iron according to manufacturer's directions.
2. In medium bowl, whisk flour, sugar, cocoa powder, baking powder, salt, and baking soda together.
3. In another bowl, beat together eggs, butter, and vanilla; add buttermilk; mix well.
4. Add wet ingredients to the dry; mix well.
5. Stir in chocolate chips just until combined.
6. Allow to rest for 5 minutes.
7. Ladle the recommended amount of waffle batter onto the center of the iron, close the iron top, and cook until the waffle is crispy on both sides and is easily removed from iron.
8. Serve immediately, or keep warm in a 200 degrees F. oven until ready to serve.

Chocolate Delights
A Collection of Chocolate Recipes
Cookbook Delights Series Book 3

Cakes

Table of Contents

Page

Best Moist Chocolate Cake

Your guests will remember this delicious chocolate cake.

Ingredients for cake:

> ¾ c. butter
> ¾ c. powdered sugar
> ½ c. self-rising flour
> 3 oz. hot chocolate mix
> 3 eggs, well beaten
> 1 Tbs. hot water

Ingredients for buttercream filling:

> ½ c. powdered sugar
> ¼ c. butter
> ¼ c. hot chocolate mix
>   water or milk, if required

Ingredients for glaze:

> ¾ c. powdered sugar
> ¼ c. hot chocolate mix
> 2 Tbs. hot water

Directions for cake:

1. Preheat oven to 350 degrees F.
2. Grease and line two 8-inch baking pans.
3. In large bowl, sift together flour and hot chocolate mix.
4. Cream butter and sugar together until light and fluffy.
5. Beat in eggs, a little at a time, adding 1 tablespoon flour mixture to prevent curdling.
6. Fold in remaining flour and chocolate mixture; stir in hot water.
7. Place mixture into prepared pans; smooth tops.
8. Bake 25 minutes, or until surface springs back when pressed lightly.
9. Remove cakes from pans.
10. Cool on wire rack.

Directions for butter cream filling:

1. Mix all ingredients together until smooth and light.
2. Spread on one of the cakes and sandwich together.

Directions for glaze:

1. Add hot water to powdered sugar and hot chocolate mix to form a thick paste.
2. Coat top of the cake before serving.
3. Use knife dipped in boiling hot water to spread icing.

Yields: 4 to 6 servings.

Chocolate Peanut Butter Chips Frosting

This is a frosting you will always enjoy with any chocolate cake in this cookbook section.

Ingredients:

1 c. powdered sugar
¼ c. butter
3 Tbs. milk
½ c. peanut butter chips
½ c. semi-sweet chocolate chips
½ tsp. vanilla extract

Directions:

1. Measure powdered sugar into medium bowl; set aside.
2. Combine butter, milk, and peanut butter chips in small saucepan; cook over low heat, stirring constantly, until chips are melted and mixture is smooth.
3. Remove from heat.
4. Add warm mixture to powdered sugar and stir in vanilla.
5. Beat until smooth.
6. Spread while frosting is warm.

Yields: 1 cup.

German Cocoa Cake

This recipe uses cocoa for that excellent German chocolate flavor.

Ingredients for cake:

¼ c. cocoa
½ c. water, boiling
1 c. plus 3 Tbs. butter, softened
2¼ c. sugar
1 tsp. vanilla extract
4 eggs
2 c. flour
1 tsp. baking soda
½ tsp. salt
1 c. buttermilk

Ingredients for coconut pecan frosting:

1½ cans sweetened condensed milk (21 oz.), not evaporated milk
6 egg yolks, slightly beaten
¾ c. butter
2 tsp. vanilla extract
1¾ c. sweetened coconut flakes
1¾ c. pecans, chopped

Directions for cake:

1. Preheat oven to 350 degrees F.
2. Grease and flour three 9-inch round baking pans.
3. In small bowl, combine cocoa and water until smooth; set aside.
4. In large bowl, beat butter, sugar, and vanilla until light and fluffy.
5. Add eggs, one at a time, beating well after each addition.

6. In medium bowl, combine flour, baking soda, and salt; mix well.
7. Add to butter mixture alternately with chocolate mixture and buttermilk, beating just enough to blend.
8. Pour batter into prepared pans.
9. Bake 25 to 30 minutes, or until top springs back when touched lightly.
10. Cool 5 minutes; remove from pans to wire racks.
11. Cool completely.

Directions for coconut pecan frosting:

1. In medium saucepan, combine milk, egg yolks, and butter.
2. Cook over low heat, stirring constantly, until mixture is thickened and bubbly.
3. Remove from heat.
4. Stir in vanilla, coconut, and pecans.
5. Cool to room temperature.
6. Note: This recipe makes extra frosting.

Yields: 10 to 12 servings.

Did You Know? . . . .

Did you know that if you live in a high altitude you can adjust your cake ingredients to turn out better cakes? The following adjustments should make the difference.

Cake High Altitude Directions:

Decrease sugar to 1¾ c.
Increase flour to 1¾ c. plus 2 Tbs.
Decrease baking powder to 1¼ tsp.
Decrease baking soda to 1¼ tsp.
Increase milk to 1 c. plus 2 Tbs.

Chocolate Raspberry Flourless Cake

This is an intense chocolate cake with subtle raspberry flavor.

Ingredients for cake:

12 pieces bittersweet or semi-sweet chocolate, chopped
¾ c. butter, unsalted, cut into pieces
6 lg. eggs, separated
6 Tbs. sugar
6 Tbs. raspberry syrup (see recipe on page 94)
2 tsp. vanilla extract

Ingredients for glaze:

½ c. whipping cream
⅓ c. dark corn syrup
3 Tbs. raspberry syrup
9 oz. bittersweet or semi-sweet chocolate, chopped

Directions for cake:

1. Preheat oven to 350 degrees F.
2. Butter a 9-inch diameter springform pan.
3. Line bottom of pan with parchment or wax paper.
4. Butter the paper; wrap outside of pan with tinfoil to prevent water from seeping in.
5. In heavy, medium saucepan, stir chocolate and butter over low heat until melted and smooth (or microwave at medium, stirring frequently).
6. Remove from heat.
7. Cool to lukewarm, stirring often.
8. Using electric mixer, beat egg yolks and sugar 3 minutes, or until very thick and pale.
9. Fold lukewarm chocolate mixture into yolk mixture.
10. Fold in vanilla.

11. In another bowl, using clean, dry beaters, beat egg whites until stiff peaks form.
12. Gradually add 6 tablespoons raspberry syrup until all is incorporated.
13. Fold egg white mixture into chocolate mixture in 3 additions.
14. Pour batter into prepared pan.
15. Bake 45 minutes, or until top is puffed and cracked, and tester inserted into center comes out with a few moist crumbs.
16. Cool cake in pan on rack. The cake will fall.
17. Gently press down on crusty top to make cake an evenly thick cake.
18. Loosen sides of pan with small knife; remove pan sides.
19. Invert cake onto serving plate and peel off parchment paper.

Directions for glaze:

1. In medium saucepan, bring cream, corn syrup, and raspberry syrup to a simmer; remove from heat.
2. Add chocolate and whisk until melted and smooth.
3. Spread ½ cup glaze over top and sides of cake.
4. Freeze 3 minutes, or until almost set.
5. Pour additional ½ cup (or remaining glaze for a more intense chocolate flavor) over cake, smooth sides, then spread on top.
6. Chill 1 hour, or until glaze is firm.
7. Serve with a dollop of sweetened whipped cream on top.
8. Garnish with chocolate shavings.

Yields: 10 servings.

Did You Know? . . . .

Did you know that seven days without chocolate makes one weak?

Chocolate Cream Filled Cake

This is a delicious dessert for the chocolate lovers in the family.

Ingredients for cake:

    2   c. flour
    1½ c. sugar
    1   c. water
    ½   c. cocoa
    ½   c. butter, softened
    3   lg. eggs
    1¼ tsp. baking powder
    1   tsp. baking soda
    1   tsp. vanilla extract

Ingredients for filling:

    ¼   c. sugar
    1   pkg. cream cheese, softened (8 oz.)
    1   lg. egg
    1   tsp. vanilla extract

Ingredients for glaze:

    1   bar white baking chocolate, broken into pieces (2 oz.)
    2   tsp. vegetable shortening, divided
    ¼   c. semi-sweet chocolate chips

Directions for cake:

1. Preheat oven to 350 degrees F.
2. Lightly grease and flour a 12-cup bundt pan.
3. In large bowl, with electric mixer on low speed, scraping bowl often, combine flour, sugar, water, cocoa, butter, egg, baking powder, baking soda, and vanilla until moistened.

4. Beat on high speed for 2 to 3 minutes, scraping bowl often, until smooth.
5. Pour 3 cups batter into prepared pan.
6. Spoon filling over batter without touching sides of pan.
7. Cover with remaining batter.
8. Bake 50 to 60 minutes, or until inserted toothpick in center comes out clean.
9. Cool in pan for 30 minutes.
10. Invert onto wire rack to cool completely.

Directions for filling:

1. In small mixer bowl, with electric mixer on low speed, combine sugar, cream cheese, egg, and vanilla; beat 2 to 3 minutes.
2. Beat another 2 to 3 minutes, scraping bowl often, until smooth.
3. Proceed as above.

Directions for glaze:

1. In small saucepan, over low heat, stirring constantly, melt chocolate and 1 teaspoon shortening until melted.
2. Drizzle over cooled cake.
3. Let stand until firm.
4. Repeat with remaining shortening and chocolate chips.
5. Store refrigerated.

Yields: 12 to 16 servings.

Did You Know? . . . .

Did you know that I am not overweight? I am chocolate-enriched.

Flourless Chocolate-Pecan Cake

This flourless chocolate cake is rich in taste and moisture.

Ingredients:

> 1 c. pecans
> 2 c. semi-sweet chocolate chips (12 oz.)
> ¾ c. butter
> 2 Tbs. orange juice
> ⅛ tsp salt
> 4 eggs
> ½ c. sugar

Ingredients for topping:

> ½ c. apricots or strawberries
> 1 Tbs. orange juice
> 1 tsp. orange peel, freshly grated
> 2 c. fresh strawberries, sliced for garnish (1 pt.)
> 1 kiwi, peeled, sliced for garnish

Directions:

1. Preheat oven to 350 degrees F.
2. Grease sides of a 9-inch springform pan.
3. Line bottom with parchment paper or wax paper.
4. Place pecans in bowl of food processor; process until finely ground.
5. In medium saucepan, combine chocolate chips and butter; cook over low heat until melted, stirring frequently.
6. Remove from heat.
7. Stir in orange juice, salt, and ground pecans.
8. In large bowl, combine eggs and sugar.

9. Beat on high speed of mixer for 3 minutes until pale yellow and slightly thickened.
10. Gently fold in chocolate mixture, blending well.
11. Pour into prepared pan.
12. Bake 35 to 38 minutes, or until inserted toothpick in center comes out with a few moist crumbs clinging to it.
13. Cake will puff and crack slightly.
14. Cool in pan on wire rack 1 hour.
15. Using knife, loosen cake from side of pan.
16. Continue to cool in pan 30 minutes; remove side of pan.
17. Invert cake onto serving plate.
18. Remove pan bottom and parchment paper.
19. Cover and refrigerate cake at least 4 hours.
20. Remove cake from refrigerator about 25 minutes before serving.
21. Prepare topping below; brush half over top of cake.
22. Garnish with fruit; spread remaining topping over fruit.
23. Cover and refrigerate leftover cake.

Directions for topping:

1. Combine apricots or strawberries, orange juice, and freshly grated orange peel in small microwave-safe bowl.
2. Microwave on high 30 seconds; stir.

Yields: 10 servings.

Did You Know? . . . .

Did you know that there actually is no caffeine in chocolate, unless it has been added? People often mistake theobromine caffeine, but they are actually two different, closely related chemicals.

One-Bowl Chocolate Cake

When I am pressed for time, this is a simple cake to make, and the orange frosting is delightful.

Ingredients for cake:

2   c. flour
1½ c. sugar
½   c. cocoa or Dutch processed cocoa
½   c. butter, softened
1   c. water
3   eggs
1¼ tsp. baking powder
1   tsp. baking soda
1   tsp. vanilla extract

Ingredients for easy orange frosting:

⅓   c. butter
2   c. powdered sugar
1   tsp. vanilla extract
½   tsp. orange extract
⅛   tsp. orange peel
2-4 Tbs. hot water
1-2 drops red and yellow food coloring (optional)

Ingredients for chocolate drizzle:

¼   c. semi-sweet chocolate chips
1½ tsp. shortening (no substitutions)

Directions for cake:

1. Preheat oven to 350 degrees F.
2. Grease a 9 x 13-inch baking pan.

3. In large bowl, place flour, sugar, cocoa, butter, water, eggs, baking powder, baking soda, and vanilla; beat until smooth.
4. Pour into prepared pan.
5. Bake 25 to 30 minutes, or until inserted toothpick in center comes out clean.
6. Cool completely in pan on wire rack.

Directions for easy orange frosting:

1. Place butter in microwave-safe bowl and microwave on high 1 minute or until melted.
2. Stir in powdered sugar, freshly grated orange peel, vanilla and orange extracts.
3. Stir in 2 to 4 tablespoons hot water for desired consistency.
4. Stir in red and yellow food color, if desired.

Directions for chocolate drizzle:

1. In small microwave-safe bowl, place semi-sweet chocolate chips and shortening.
2. Microwave on high 15 to 30 seconds; stir.
3. If necessary, microwave on high additional 15 seconds at a time, stirring after each heating, just until chips are melted and mixture is smooth.

Yields: 12 to 16 servings.

Did You Know? . . . .

Did you know that a research study found that women who ate chocolate bars three or four times a week were no more prone to heart disease than women who rarely ate chocolate?

Chocolate Cake with Strawberries

Try this delicious chocolate cake with strawberries!

Ingredients:

- 1 c. water, boiling
- 1½ tsp. instant espresso or 1 Tbs. instant coffee granules
- 1¾ c. flour
- 2 c. sugar
- ¾ c. unsweetened cocoa
- 2 tsp. baking soda
- 1 tsp. baking powder
- 1 tsp. salt
- 1 c. buttermilk
- 2 eggs, well beaten
- ⅓ c. canola oil
- 1 tsp. vanilla extract
- 1 c. whipping cream, whipped
- 2 c. strawberries, sliced

Directions:

1. Preheat oven to 350 degrees F.
2. Lightly grease and flour two 9-inch round baking pans.
3. In small bowl, combine water and espresso.
4. In large bowl, combine flour, sugar, cocoa, baking soda, baking powder, and salt; mix well.
5. Add buttermilk, eggs, oil, and vanilla to cooled espresso mixture; mix well.
6. Add to sugar mixture.
7. With electric mixer on medium speed, beat until well blended.
8. Pour batter into prepared baking pans.
9. Bake 45 minutes, or until inserted toothpick in center comes out clean.
10. Cool in pans 10 minutes.
11. Remove from pans to wire racks.
12. Cool completely.

13. Place 1 cake layer on a plate; spread with 1 cup whipped cream.
14. Top with other cake layer.
15. Spread remaining whipped cream over top of cake.
16. Arrange strawberries on top of cake.
17. Store cake loosely covered in refrigerator.

Yields: 16 servings.

Chocolate Lava Cake

This chocolate cake is all the rage at trendy restaurants. Just crack it open to find a lovely, gooey center.

Ingredients:

½ lb. bittersweet chocolate, finely chopped
½ lb. butter, unsalted
6 eggs
1½ c. sugar
½ c. flour

Directions:

1. Preheat oven to 400 degrees F.
2. Butter bottom and sides of 15 four-ounce ramekins.
3. Sprinkle with sugar, tapping to remove extra sugar.
4. In double boiler, melt chocolate and butter.
5. Whisk until thoroughly melted.
6. In large bowl, whisk eggs, sugar, and flour together until just blended.
7. Gradually whisk chocolate into egg mixture.
8. Evenly divide the mixture between the prepared ramekins, using about ⅓ cup for each.
9. Place ramekins on a baking sheet.
10. Bake 10 to 12 minutes, or until the tops are firm and beginning to crack, and the edges are set.
11. Remove from oven,
12. Serve immediately with ice cream.

Yields: 15 servings.

Fudge Cake with Fudge Frosting

Caleb loves chocolate fudge cake and often requests this for his birthday parties. This is very rich, but easy to make. It has also been a family request for many dinners as well as special occasions.

Ingredients for fudge cake:

¾ c. butter, melted
1½ c. sugar
1½ tsp. vanilla extract
3   egg yolks
½ c. plus 1 Tbs. cocoa powder
½ c. flour
3   Tbs. canola oil
3   Tbs. water
¼ c. pecans, finely chopped
3   egg whites at room temperature
⅛ tsp. cream of tartar
⅛ tsp. salt
     pecan halves

Ingredients for chocolate fudge icing:

1⅓ c. semi-sweet chocolate chips
½ c. heavy cream or whipping cream

Directions for fudge cake:

1. Preheat oven to 350 degrees F.
2. Line bottom of 9-inch springform pan with aluminum foil.
3. Butter foil and sides of pan; set aside.
4. In large bowl, combine melted butter, sugar, and vanilla; beat well.
5. Add egg yolks, one at a time, beating well after each addition.

6. Blend in cocoa, flour, oil, and water; beat well.
7. Stir in chopped pecans.
8. In small mixer bowl, beat egg whites, cream of tartar, and salt until stiff peaks form.
9. Carefully fold into chocolate mixture.
10. Spoon into prepared pan.
11. Bake 45 minutes, or until top begins to crack slightly.
12. Note: Cake will not be completely done in center.
13. Cool for 1 hour.
14. Cover.
15. Refrigerate; chill until firm.
16. Remove sides of pan.

Directions for chocolate fudge icing:

1. In small saucepan, combine chocolate chips and cream.
2. Cook over low heat, stirring constantly, until chocolate melts and mixture is smooth; do not boil.
3. Cut cake into 12 slices.
4. Remove foil from bottom.
5. Place each slice of cake on a serving plate.
6. Pour icing over each cake slice; allow to run down the sides of each portion.
7. Garnish with pecan halves.
8. Slice at serving time.
9. Note: You can also pour the icing over the entire cake, and garnish with pecan halves.
10. Allow to cool before serving.

Did You Know? . . . .

Did you know that flowers wilt, jewelry tarnishes, and candles burn out...but chocolate doesn't hang around long enough to get old?

Very Chocolate Cake

This is a very delicious and rich chocolate cake with a fudge filling and ganache frosting or you can you're your favorite.

Ingredients for cake:

2   c. cake flour, sifted
2   tsp. baking powder
½   tsp. baking soda
½   tsp. salt
3   sq. unsweetened chocolate
⅔   c. water
1½ c. sugar, divided
1   tsp. vanilla extract
⅔   c. butter, softened
3   eggs
⅓   c. buttermilk

Ingredients for chocolate fudge filling:

6   sq. semi-sweet chocolate (1 oz. ea.)
3   Tbs. butter
7   Tbs. milk
1   tsp. vanilla extract
3   c. powdered sugar, sifted

Ingredients for ganache frosting:

1   lb. fine-quality semi-sweet chocolate (Callebaut)
1   c. heavy cream
2   Tbs. sugar
2   Tbs. light corn syrup
¼   c. butter, cut into pieces

Directions for cake:

1. Preheat oven to 350 degrees F.
2. Lightly grease and flour two 8-inch round baking pans.
3. On wax paper, sift flour, baking powder, baking soda, and salt; set aside.

4. In small saucepan, over low heat, stirring constantly, cook chocolate, water, and ¼ cup sugar until thick and smooth.
5. Transfer to bowl; chill over ice water, stirring often.
6. Add vanilla.
7. In large bowl, beat butter and remaining sugar until fluffy.
8. Beat in eggs, one at a time.
9. Add chilled chocolate mixture; blend.
10. Add sifted ingredients alternately with buttermilk, beating well after each addition, until smooth.
11. Pour into prepared baking pans.
12. Bake 35 minutes, or until inserted toothpick in center comes out clean.
13. Remove from pans; cool on wire rack.
14. Split in half if desired.
15. Fill and frost with chocolate fudge filling.

Directions for chocolate fudge filling:

1. In small saucepan, combine chocolate and butter.
2. Place over very low heat just until melted.
3. Transfer to bowl; beat in milk and vanilla until blended.
4. Gradually beat in powdered sugar until smooth and spreadable.

Directions for ganache frosting:

1. Finely chop chocolate.
2. In 1½ to 2-quart saucepan, bring cream, sugar, and corn syrup to boil over moderately low heat, whisking until sugar is dissolved.
3. Remove from heat; add chocolate, whisking until chocolate is melted.
4. Add butter pieces to frosting; whisk until smooth.
5. Transfer to a bowl; cool, stirring occasionally, until spreadable.
6. Note: If desired, place bowl in refrigerator for awhile, stirring occasionally until it cools to your desired consistency.
7. Spread on top and sides of cake layers.

Deep Dark Chocolate Cake

Dark chocolate is the ultimate for a chocolate cake.

Ingredients:

    2   c. sugar
    1¾ c. flour
    ¾   c. cocoa or Dutch processed cocoa
    1½ tsp. baking powder
    1½ tsp. baking soda
    1   tsp. salt
    2   eggs
    1   c. milk
    ½   c. canola oil
    2   tsp. vanilla extract
    1   c. water, boiling

Directions:

1. Preheat oven to 350 degrees F.
2. Grease and flour two 9-inch round pans or one 9 x 13-inch baking pan.
3. In large bowl, combine sugar, flour, cocoa, baking powder, baking soda, and salt.
4. Add eggs, milk, oil, and vanilla; beat on medium speed of electric mixer for 2 minutes.
5. Stir in boiling water (batter will be thin).
6. Pour batter into prepared pans.
7. Bake 30 to 35 minutes for round pans, 35 to 40 minutes for rectangular pan, or until inserted toothpick in center comes out clean.
8. Cool 10 minutes; remove from pans to wire racks.
9. Cool completely. (Cake may be left in rectangular pan, if desired.)

Yields: 8 to 10 servings.

Did You Know? . . . .

Did you know that chocolate doesn't make the world go around? But it certainly makes the ride worthwhile.

Chocolate Delights
A Collection of Chocolate Recipes
Cookbook Delights Series Book 3

Candies

Table of Contents

Page

Almond Joys

If you like coconut, you'll love these. It really does taste like an Almond Joy.

Ingredients:

   4 c. coconut, shredded (8½ oz.)
   ¼ c. light corn syrup
   1 pkg. milk chocolate pieces (11½ oz.)
   ¼ c. white vegetable shortening
   26 almonds, whole, natural

Directions:

1. Line 2 large baking sheets with wax paper.
2. Set large wire cooling rack on paper; set aside.
3. Place coconut in large bowl; set aside.
4. Place corn syrup in 1-cup glass measure and microwave 1 minute until syrup boils.
5. Immediately pour over coconut.
6. Work warm syrup into coconut using the back of a wooden spoon until coconut is thoroughly coated.
7. Using 1 level measuring tablespoon of coconut, shape and roll into balls.
8. Place on wire rack and let dry 10 minutes.
9. Reroll coconut balls so there are no loose ends of coconut sticking up.
10. Place milk chocolate and shortening in a 4-cup glass measure or 1½-quart microwave-safe bowl.
11. Microwave 2 minutes until smooth and glossy.
12. Working quickly, spoon 1 level measuring tablespoon of chocolate over each coconut ball, making sure chocolate coats and letting excess chocolate drip down onto wax paper.
13. While chocolate coating is still soft, lightly press whole almond on top of each.
14. Let stand to set or place in refrigerator.
15. Store in a single layer in airtight container.

Best Chocolate Fudge

This fudge recipe is the best I have tried. It is creamy with great tasting chocolate, and packed with walnuts. Try using milk chocolate or dark chocolate to suit your taste. This is another family favorite.

Ingredients:

    2¼ c. top quality chocolate chips, room temperature
    3   c. fresh walnuts, chopped in large pieces
    1   lg. can evaporated milk
    1   jar marshmallow crème, room temperature (9 oz.)
    3   tsp. vanilla extract
    1   c. butter, room temperature
    4½ c. sugar

Directions:

1. Butter a 9 x 13 x 2-inch baking pan.
2. Cover with wax paper; butter wax paper as well.
3. In large bowl, combine chocolate, walnuts, marshmallow crème, vanilla, and butter; mix well.
4. In large saucepan, combine milk and sugar.
5. Over very low heat, bring to rolling boil.
6. Continue to boil for 11 minutes, stirring constantly with wooden spoon. It may turn brown, but don't be alarmed.
7. Pour over chocolate mixture; mix quickly. Do not beat.
8. Pour into wax paper-covered pan.
9. Important: Get mixture out of bowl and into pan as rapidly as possible.
10. Do not make substitutions for ingredients.

Did You Know? . . . .

Did you know that there is so much chocolate and so little time?

Blobs

These were one of my favorite sweet treats when I was a child. My aunt used to make them for me, and they were a hit when I brought them to group meetings for children.

Ingredients:

- 1 c. white corn syrup
- 1 c. sugar
- 7 c. Special K cereal
- 1 c. creamy peanut butter
- 1 c. butter
- 1 c. butterscotch chips
- 1 c. chocolate chips

Directions:

1. Well butter a 9 x 13-inch baking pan.
2. In large saucepan, bring syrup and sugar just to a boil.
3. Add cereal and peanut butter; mix well.
4. In small saucepan, melt butter, butterscotch, and chocolate chips.
5. Pour over cereal mixture.
6. Place into prepared pan or drop by spoonfuls on wax paper.

Butterfinger Candy

This candy is so easy to make, and it is delicious.

Ingredients:

- 1 c. peanut butter
- ⅓ c. white corn syrup
- 1 c. sugar
- ½ c. water
- 3 chocolate candy bars

Directions:

1. Lightly butter a 9 x 9-inch baking pan.
2. Cook sugar, corn syrup, and water over medium heat to 305 degrees F. on candy thermometer.
3. Stir in peanut butter; pour into prepared pan.
4. While still hot, place 3 chocolate bars on top and spread evenly.
5. Refrigerate; when set, break into pieces.

Caramel Frosting Fudge

This recipe was given to me by Carol Spitzer. This is a very rich and wonderful fudge. It can be used as fudge or a frosting.

Ingredients:

4 lb. dark brown sugar
4 c. white sugar
4 c. cream or evaporated milk
½ c. corn syrup
1 c. butter
1 Tbs. plus 1 tsp. vanilla extract

Directions:

1. Lightly butter a baking pan.
2. In large saucepan, combine both sugars, cream, corn syrup, and butter.
3. Stirring on medium-high heat, bring to a boil.
4. Reduce heat to medium and stop stirring.
5. Continue to boil until candy reaches 230 degrees F. at soft-ball stage.
6. Remove from heat and add vanilla.
7. Beat until it loses its shine.
8. Pour immediately into prepared pan.
9. Allow to set up.
10. Cut into squares.

Chocolate-Covered Cherries

This is a recipe you need to make at least a week ahead of time in order to let the fondant filling liquefy.

Ingredients:

 2   c. maraschino cherries, drained (1.5-lb. jar)
 ¼ c. butter, softened
 1   Tbs. light corn syrup
 3   c. powdered sugar
 3   lb. dark chocolate, finely chopped
 1-2 tsp. cherry liqueur (optional for adults)

Directions:

1. Drain cherries, reserving liquid for later.
2. Place cherries on a cooling rack that has been set over a baking sheet or wax paper.
3. Allow cherries to dry overnight.
4. In large mixing bowl, with electric mixer on medium speed, beat butter, corn syrup, and 2 tablespoons reserved cherry liquid until smooth and velvety.
5. Turn mixer to low, and slowly sift in powdered sugar, scraping down the bowl as necessary.
6. Mix until well incorporated.
7. If mixture is too sticky, add a bit more powdered sugar; if it is too stiff, add a bit more cherry juice.
8. You should end up with a pale pink mixture the consistency of slightly soft butter.
9. This is your fondant filling.
10. Scoop up an almond-size ball of fondant with a spoon, and roll it in your hands to get a rough ball.
11. Flatten ball between your palms, and place a dried cherry in the center of the fondant.
12. Bring together outer edges; pinch to seal the fondant over the cherry, making sure it is covered completely.

13. Repeat with remaining cherries and fondant.
14. Place your fondant-covered cherries in the refrigerator for 30 minutes to firm up.
15. Temper the chocolate, and prepare a place in your kitchen to dip the cherries.
16. Line a baking sheet with foil or wax paper.
17. Dip cherries in the chocolate, using two forks or a candy dipping fork.
18. Drag the cherry over the lip of the bowl to remove excess chocolate, and carefully place on prepared baking sheet.
19. Repeat with remaining fondant balls; place in the refrigerator to firm up for 30 minutes.
20. Dip cherries in chocolate again, following the same method as above.
21. This second dipping is necessary to produce a solid outer shell that will prevent the liquid filling from escaping.
22. Refrigerate 30 minutes, or until firm.
23. Place the cherries in an airtight container and store in the refrigerator for at least a week.
24. At the end of this time, the center should be liquid and you have gourmet homemade chocolate-covered cherries.
25. If you can't wait a week, they are also good freshly made, but with a firmer center.
26. Variation: These cherries are great for the entire family. If you would like a more grown-up version, add 1 to 2 teaspoons cherry liqueur, depending on taste, in with the cherry liquid when you are beating the fondant.

Did You Know? . . . .

Did you know what life without chocolate would be? It would be like a beach without water!

Chocolate-Covered Pretzels

This is a very easy-to-make recipe to enjoy with your family. My nephew Derek always requested this treat for the holidays.

Ingredients:

12 oz. milk chocolate (or dark, or white), finely chopped
2 Tbs. solid vegetable shortening or cocoa butter
6-8 oz. small, salted pretzels

Directions:

1. To garnish, get a small amount of grated or shaved chocolate (in contrasting color from the color of the chocolate in which you dip the pretzels) or chocolate sprinkle.
2. Line several baking sheets with aluminum foil, shiny side up.
3. In a medium heatproof bowl, combine chopped chocolate and shortening.
4. Set over hot water on low heat.
5. Stir or whisk frequently until melted and smooth.
6. Milk and white chocolates, even those of good quality, are often stubborn about melting. If yours won't melt smoothly, turn it into the work bowl of a food processor fitted with a steel blade. Be careful not to get any water into the chocolate.
7. Process just until smooth.
8. Carefully turn melted chocolate into a small bowl.
9. If necessary, cool, stirring often, until just slightly warm.
10. Place one pretzel in the melted chocolate.
11. With a three or four-tined fork, gently push the pretzel just under the surface of the chocolate to cover it completely.
12. Pick up the pretzel so that it lies flat on the fork tines.
13. Using short up and down motions, gently shake off excess chocolate from the pretzel.

14. Carefully place the dipped pretzel on a foil-lined baking sheet.
15. Continue dipping, placing the dipped pretzels close together on the foil-lined sheet.
16. Excess chocolate may form small pools where a pretzel touches the sheet, but these should be minimal in size.
17. After dipping every 5 or 6 pretzels, sprinkle the ones you've just dipped with a small pinch of the grated or shaved chocolate or chocolate sprinkles.
18. Keep the decorations dainty and sparse, and sprinkle around the top of the dipped pretzels, not all in one place.
19. When one sheet has been filled up, place it into the refrigerator just until the chocolate covering on the pretzels has hardened; this shouldn't take more than 10 to 20 minutes.
20. Test by peeling several pretzels from the sheet, using a tissue or sheet of paper towel to protect the chocolate covering on the pretzels from your fingers.
21. The chocolate covering should look dull and dry, not shiny and wet, and you should be able to peel the pretzels easily from the foil-lined sheet.
22. When chocolate covering has set, remove pretzels from refrigerator.
23. Gently peel from foil-lined baking sheet; store in airtight container.
24. Note: As you are dipping, the chocolate may cool and thicken too much to enable you to dip the pretzels easily. If so, reheat gently over hot water on low heat (water should not touch the bottom of chocolate bowl), stirring often, just until slightly warm.
25. It might also be helpful to transfer the melted chocolate mixture into progressively smaller bowls as you dip.
26. Do not try to use up the last bit of melted chocolate; the dipped pretzels won't look as smooth (this is a good place to use the smaller pieces and crumbs for a cook's treat).
27. Store dipped pretzels in airtight container in a cool room.

Cathedral Windows

This recipe is delicious and gives your candy dish a very festive looking variety.

Ingredients:

¼ lb. butter
1 pkg. semi-sweet chocolate chips
1 c. walnuts, chopped
12 oz. miniature marshmallows, colored
7 oz. sweetened coconut, grated

Directions:

1. Heat butter and chocolate chips in top of double boiler over low heat, stirring occasionally until melted and smooth.
2. Remove from heat and cool slightly.
3. Toss marshmallows and nuts in a large bowl.
4. Stir chocolate into marshmallow-nut mixture.
5. Tear 5 sheets of wax paper, nine inches each.
6. Divide dough into fifths and place each fifth on a sheet of wax paper.
7. Sprinkle each generously with coconut.
8. Roll tightly into 2-inch diameter logs using the wax paper to keep tubes even.
9. Refrigerate overnight or until firm.
10. Before serving, remove wax paper and cut into ½-inch slices.

Yields: 60 servings.

Chocolate Mints

These are so good, and only take a few minutes to make.

Ingredients:

1 pkg. cream cheese (8 oz.)
½ c. butter

¼ c. cocoa
1 tsp. peppermint extract
¼ c. heavy cream
½ c. sugar

Directions:

1. Put cream cheese and butter in a microwave for 1 minute to soften.
2. Place in bowl; add remaining ingredients; blend well.
3. Spoon into paper cups and chill.

Chocolate Peanut Butter Fudge

I enjoy peanut butter with my chocolate as much as my guests.

Ingredients:

3 c. sugar
1 c. evaporated milk
¼ c. cocoa
½ c. peanut butter
1 Tbs. butter

Directions:

1. Butter a 9 x 9-inch baking pan.
2. Combine sugar, evaporated milk, and cocoa in saucepan.
3. Stir over high heat until mixture comes to a rolling boil.
4. Reduce heat to medium and continue cooking to a soft-ball stage.
5. Remove from heat; add peanut butter and butter.
6. Beat by hand until creamy; pour into prepared pan.
7. Allow to cool and cut into squares.

Chocolate Butter Fudge

This is one of the versions of fudge that my mom liked to make. It is a variety that requires beating to finish it, but it is worth the extra trouble.

Ingredients:

- 3 c. sugar
- 1 pkg. unflavored gelatin
- 1 c. milk
- ½ c. corn syrup, light
- 3 sq. unsweetened chocolate (3 oz.)
- 1¼ c. butter
- 2 tsp. vanilla extract
- 1¼ c. walnuts, chopped

Directions:

1. In 3½-quart saucepan, mix sugar and gelatin together.
2. Stir in milk, corn syrup, chocolate, and butter; mix well.
3. Over medium heat, cook, stirring frequently, to 238 degrees F. on candy thermometer, or until a little mixture in cold water forms a soft ball that flattens when removed from water.
4. Remove from heat.
5. Pour into large bowl.
6. Stir in vanilla.
7. Cool 20 minutes.
8. Beat with wooden spoon until candy thickens.
9. Stir in walnuts.
10. Spread in prepared pan.
11. Cool; cut into squares.

Yields: 2½ lbs.

Chocolate Raspberry Truffles

The most beloved of French candies, truffles, are fast becoming one of our favorites too. Our version has an optional cocoa powder dusting or a crunchy hazelnut outer coating.

Ingredients:

¾ c. butter, unsalted
1 lb. semi-sweet chocolate, finely chopped
½ c. seedless raspberry jam
¼ c. black raspberry liqueur or raspberry Chambord
½ c. Dutch process cocoa powder (optional)
1 c. hazelnuts, roasted, finely chopped

Directions:

1. Cut butter into pieces; melt in top of double boiler or metal bowl over (but not touching) hot water.
2. Add chocolate, stirring occasionally until smooth.
3. Remove from heat.
4. Blend in raspberry jam and liqueur until smooth.
5. Cover; freeze until firm, about 2 hours; or refrigerate until firm, 4 hours or overnight.
6. Place cocoa or hazelnuts in a wide shallow pie pan.
7. Using a melon baller or a tablespoon, scoop a tablespoon of cold chocolate mixture between your palms and roll to form a round ball.
8. Roll in desired coating; place on sided baking sheet.
9. Repeat until all the chocolate mixture is gone.
10. Cover tightly with plastic wrap until ready to serve.
11. Remove from refrigerator about 10 minutes before serving.
12. This recipe may be prepared up to 5 days ahead if truffles are covered tightly and refrigerated.
13. May be frozen for up to a month, double wrapped in plastic.

Chocolate Truffles

You will love these truffles with all the variations.

Ingredients:

¾ c. butter
¾ c. cocoa
1 can sweetened condensed milk (14 oz.)
1 Tbs. vanilla extract
cocoa or powdered sugar (for rolling truffles in)
nuts, chopped (optional for rolling truffles in)

Directions:

1. Melt butter in heavy saucepan over low heat.
2. Add cocoa; stir until smooth.
3. Add sweetened condensed milk; cook and stir constantly until mixture is thick, smooth, and glossy, about 4 minutes.
4. Remove from heat; stir in vanilla.
5. Cover; refrigerate 3 to 4 hours or until firm.
6. Shape into 1¼-inch balls; place on wax paper-lined baking sheet.
7. Roll in cocoa, powdered sugar, or chopped nuts.
8. Refrigerate until firm, 1 to 2 hours.
9. Store, covered, in refrigerator.

Additional ingredients for nut truffle variation:

¾ c. pecans, toasted and chopped

Directions for nut truffle variation:

1. Add chopped and toasted pecans to chocolate mixture when adding vanilla.

Additional ingredients for rum nut truffle variation:

2-3 Tbs. rum or 1 tsp. rum extract
¾ c. nuts, chopped

Directions for rum nut truffle variation:

1. Decrease vanilla to 1 teaspoon.
2. Stir in rum or rum extract and nuts.

Additional ingredients for espresso truffle variation:

1¼ tsp. powdered instant espresso or instant coffee

Directions for espresso truffle variation:

1. Decrease vanilla to 1 teaspoon.
2. Stir in instant coffee when adding vanilla.
3. Roll balls in cocoa or chopped nuts.

Turtles

This recipe is from my sister Sandy. She liked making these for friends and family. They were always enjoyed by everyone.

Ingredients:

70 caramels
5   Tbs. cream
4½ c. pecans
2   giant chocolate bars
½   bar paraffin wax

Directions:

1. Melt caramels and cream in double boiler; add pecans.
2. Drop by teaspoons on greased baking sheet and freeze.
3. Melt chocolate bars and then add paraffin wax.
4. Dip frozen candy into chocolate and put on baking sheet.

Yields: about 40.

Mint Fondant

I remember my mother making these after-dinner mint candies when I was a little girl. Making fondant is easier each time you make it, and there is no end to the flavorings and colors.

Ingredients for fondant:

2½ c. sugar
⅓ c. corn syrup
2   Tbs. butter
⅛ tsp. salt
1   c. water
1   tsp. peppermint flavoring

Ingredients for chocolate coating:

2   sm. pkg. semi-sweet chocolate chips
1   sm. pkg. milk chocolate chips

Directions for fondant:

1. In a saucepan, stir together sugar, salt, corn syrup, and water while bringing it to boil.
2. Wash down sides of pan, cover, and cook 3 minutes.
3. Uncover and finish cooking until small amount forms a soft ball in cold water (237 degrees F.).
4. Pour out on wet platter and cool to lukewarm.
5. Work with paddle or spoon until white and creamy.
6. Add peppermint and coloring and knead until smooth.
7. Place in bowl, cover with damp cloth, and let set for 1 hour.
8. Use powdered sugar for kneading and shaping.
9. Roll out on wax paper into a sheet ¼-inch thick.
10. Leave on wax paper until outside is slightly hardened.
11. Cover with chocolate coating on next page.

Directions for chocolate coating:

1. In double boiler, mix and stir both chocolate chips together until melted and well blended.
2. Cover 1 side of fondant with chocolate and let set.
3. After chocolate has set, turn fondant over and coat the opposite side.
4. After chocolate has set, cut into rectangles or other desired shapes.

Homemade Almond Roca

This is a recipe that I received from Carol Spitzer. It is a homemade version of the boughten candy, and it is delicious.

Ingredients:

2 c. brown sugar (1 lb.)
1 tsp. salt
½ c. water
1 c. butter
1 lg. chocolate candy bar
1 c. almonds, chopped (optional)

Directions:

1. Butter a large baking sheet.
2. In large saucepan, combine brown sugar, salt, water, and butter.
3. Over medium heat, cook 8 minutes, stirring constantly to hard-crack stage, 300 degrees F. on candy thermometer.
4. Reduce heat to low; cook 10 minutes more.
5. Remove from heat.
6. Stir in chopped almonds if desired.
7. Pour very quickly into prepared baking sheet.
8. Cool.
9. In small microwave-safe bowl, melt chocolate bar.
10. Cover both sides of candies in melted chocolate.

Chocolate-Covered Almond Apricots

Chocolate-covered almond apricots are delicious, and worth the time to make them. These can be stored in the refrigerator, but they won't last long, as they are both delicious and rich.

Ingredients:

- 2 c. vanilla wafer crumbs, crushed (60 wafers)
- 1 c. almonds, finely chopped
- ⅓ c. cocoa
- 1 can sweetened condensed milk (14 oz.)
- 1 pkg. dried apricots, chopped (8 oz.)
- ½ c. candied cherries, chopped
- ¼ tsp. almond extract
- 2 c. milk chocolate chips (11½ oz.)
- 4 tsp. shortening (no substitutions) or canola oil

Directions

1. Line small muffin cups (1¾-inch diameter) with paper baking cups.
2. In large bowl, combine crumbs, almonds, and cocoa.
3. Add milk, apricots, cherries, and almond extract; mix well.
4. Refrigerate 30 minutes.
5. Roll mixture into 1-inch balls.
6. Press into prepared muffin cups.
7. Place chocolate chips and shortening in medium microwave-safe bowl.
8. Microwave on high 1½ minutes; stir.
9. If necessary, microwave on high an additional 15 seconds at a time, stirring after each heating, just until chips are melted when stirred.
10. Spoon 1 teaspoonful melted chocolate over each filled cup.
11. Refrigerate until chocolate is set.
12. Store, covered, in refrigerator.

Yields: 6 dozen candies.

Chocolate Delights

A Collection of Chocolate Recipes
Cookbook Delights Series Book 3

Cookies

Table of Contents

Page

Butternut Ball Cookies

Use powdered sugar rather than granulated sugar to make these cookies more tender.

Ingredients:

> 1   c. butter, softened
> ¾   c. powdered sugar, sifted
> 2   tsp. vanilla extract
> 2⅓ c. flour
> ¼   tsp. salt
>   pecan halves
>   chocolate kisses

Directions:

1. Preheat oven to 400 degrees F.
2. In large bowl, combine butter and powdered sugar.
3. Mix well.
4. Add vanilla and beat.
5. Add dry ingredients and mix until a dough forms.
6. Form dough around pecan halves or chocolate kisses, enclosing nut or chocolate completely.
7. Bake 10 to 12 minutes on ungreased baking sheets.
8. Cookies should not brown.
9. Immediately drop into a bowl full of powdered sugar and roll to coat.
10. Let cool on wire racks.
11. When cool, roll in powdered sugar again.

No Bake Cookies

These chocolate-dipped cookies are quick to make for such an elegant and delicious result.

Ingredients:

> 1   c. peanut butter
> 1   pt. marshmallow crème

1½ c. crispy rice cereal
1 tsp. vanilla extract
½ c. powdered sugar
1 lg. chocolate bar

Directions:

1. In large bowl, mix ingredients thoroughly and shape into balls.
2. Place in freezer for 20 minutes.
3. Melt chocolate bar in microwave.
4. Dip balls in melted chocolate.

Chocolate Coconut Cookies (No Bake)

These are easy to make and children and adults all seem to enjoy them, as they disappear quickly.

Ingredients:

1¾ c. sugar
6 Tbs. cocoa powder, unsweetened
¾ c. evaporated milk
½ c. butter
½ tsp. vanilla extract
1¾ c. coconut, sweetened, shredded
3 c. rolled oats

Directions:

1. In medium saucepan, combine sugar, cocoa, evaporated milk, and butter.
2. Over medium heat, cook and stir, until mixture comes to a boil.
3. Boil 1 minute, stirring constantly.
4. Remove from heat; stir in vanilla.
5. Add rolled oats and coconut; mix well.
6. Drop by tablespoons onto baking sheet lined with wax paper.
7. Refrigerate until firm.

Chewy Chocolate Pan Cookies

These pan cookies are so yummy they disappear as fast as you can make them.

Ingredients:

- 1¼ c. butter, softened
- 2 c. sugar
- 2 eggs
- 2 tsp. vanilla extract
- 2 c. flour
- ¾ c. cocoa
- 1 tsp. baking soda
- ½ tsp. salt
- 1⅔ c. peanut butter chips (10 oz.)

Directions:

1. Preheat oven to 350 degrees F.
2. Grease a 15½ x 10½ x 1-inch jellyroll pan.
3. In large bowl, beat butter and sugar until light and fluffy.
4. Add eggs and vanilla; beat well.
5. In medium bowl, combine flour, cocoa, baking soda, and salt; gradually blend into butter mixture.
6. Stir in peanut butter chips.
7. Spread batter into prepared pan.
8. Bake 20 minutes, or until set.
9. Cool completely in pan on wire rack.
10. Cut into bars.

Yields: 48 bars.

Did You Know? . . . .

Did you know why there is no Chocoholics Anonymous? No one wants to quit eating chocolate!

Chocolate Chip Cookies

It's hard to replace an old-fashioned chocolate chip cookie on any cookie list.

Ingredients:

1 c. butter
¾ c. white sugar
¾ c. brown sugar
2 eggs
2 tsp. vanilla extract
2¼ c. flour
1 tsp. baking soda
1 tsp. salt
2 c. milk chocolate chips

Directions:

1. Preheat oven to 350 degrees F.
2. Grease baking sheet.
3. In large bowl, cream butter and both sugars until light and fluffy.
4. Add eggs, one at a time, beating well after each addition.
5. Stir in vanilla.
6. In medium bowl, combine flour, baking soda, and salt; gradually stir into creamed mixture.
7. Fold in chocolate chips.
8. Drop by rounded teaspoonfuls onto prepared baking sheet.
9. Bake 8 to 10 minutes, or until light brown.
10. Cool 5 minutes on baking sheet.
11. Remove to wire rack to cool completely.

Did You Know? . . . .

Did you know that in the cookies of life, friends are the chocolate chips?

Chocolate and Raspberry Bars

These bar cookies are so good it is hard to keep from having them for breakfast.

Ingredients:

1½ c. flour
½ c. sugar
½ tsp. baking powder
½ tsp. salt
½ c. butter, softened
1 egg, beaten
¼ c. milk
¼ tsp. vanilla extract
¾ c. raspberry preserves
1 c. semi-sweet chocolate chips

Directions:

1. Preheat oven to 400 degrees F.
2. Grease a 9 x 13-inch baking pan.
3. In large bowl, combine flour, sugar, baking powder, and salt.
4. Cut in butter until mixture resembles coarse crumbs.
5. Add egg, milk, and vanilla; beat on medium speed of mixer until well blended.
6. Reserve ½ cup mixture for topping.
7. Spread remaining mixture onto bottom of prepared pan (this will be a very thin layer).
8. Spread preserves evenly over dough; sprinkle chocolate chips over top.
9. Drop reserved dough by half teaspoonfuls over chocolate chips.
10. Bake 25 minutes, or until golden brown.
11. Cool completely in pan on wire rack.
12. Cut into bars.

Chocolate Pecan Bars

These chocolate pecan bar cookies are wonderful. They are easy to make and will disappear quickly.

Ingredients:

    1¼ c. flour
    1   c. powdered sugar
    ½   c. cocoa
    1   c. butter, cold
    1   can sweetened condensed milk (14 oz.)
    1   egg
    2   tsp. vanilla extract
    1½ c. pecans, chopped

Directions:

1. Preheat oven to 350 degrees F (325 degrees F. for glass dish).
2. In large bowl, combine flour, sugar, and cocoa.
3. Cut in butter until crumbly.
4. Press firmly onto bottom of ungreased 9 x 13-inch baking pan.
5. Bake 15 minutes; remove from oven.
6. In medium bowl, beat milk, egg, and vanilla until well blended.
7. Stir in pecans.
8. Spread mixture evenly over hot baked crust.
9. Return to oven.
10. Bake 25 minutes, or until lightly browned.
11. Cool completely in pan on wire rack.
12. Cut into bars.
13. Cover.
14. Store in refrigerator.

Yields: 36 bars.

Chocolate Crusted Coconut Bars

These are great bars with a combination of chocolate and delicious coconut.

Ingredients for crust:

   1½ c. flour
   ¼   c. sugar
   2   Tbs. cocoa powder, unsweetened
   8   Tbs. butter, unsalted, room temperature

Ingredients for macaroons:

   4   c. coconut flakes, unsweetened
   8   lg. egg whites
   2   c. powdered sugar
   ½   c. sweetened coconut cream
   2   oz. bittersweet chocolate, melted for decorating

Directions for crust:

   1. Move oven rack to middle of oven.
   2. Preheat oven to 375 degrees F.
   3. Lightly grease a 9 x 13-inch baking pan.
   4. Place flour, sugar, and cocoa in a bowl.
   5. Add butter bit by bit, thoroughly blending.
   6. Between 2 sheets of parchment paper, roll dough into a 9 x 13-inch rectangle.
   7. Peel off 1 sheet of parchment.
   8. Fit dough into bottom of prepared pan.
   9. Peel off another sheet of parchment.
   10. Prick holes in dough with fork.
   11. Refrigerate while making the macaroons.

Directions for macaroons:

   1. In medium bowl, mix coconut, egg whites, sugar, and cream together.
   2. Lightly press mixture over crust.
   3. Bake 15 minutes, or until golden brown.

4. Set on wire rack to cool.
5. Cut into 3 x 3-inch bars.
6. Drizzle with melted chocolate.

Chocolate Peanut Butter Cookies

I enjoy peanut butter and chocolate cookies as much as anyone I know – including my children.

Ingredients:

½ c. butter
½ c. peanut butter
½ c. sugar
½ c. brown sugar
1 egg
1 c. flour
½ tsp. baking soda
½ tsp. baking powder
¼ tsp. salt
1 pkg. chocolate chips

Directions:

1. Preheat oven to 325 degrees F.
2. Lightly grease a baking sheet.
3. In large bowl, cream butter, peanut butter, and sugars.
4. Beat in egg; mix well.
5. In medium bowl, sift flour, baking soda, baking powder, and salt together.
6. Add dry ingredients to creamed mixture; mix well.
7. Stir in chocolate chips.
8. Roll into balls, or drop by teaspoons onto prepared baking sheet.
9. Flatten slightly with sugar-dipped fork.
10. Bake 15 to 20 minutes, or until done.

Yields: 3½ dozen.

Chocolate Chip Fruit Nut Bars

Chocolate chips add rich chocolate flavor to these dried fruit and nut bars. They are rich, and make a delicious treat.

Ingredients:

- ½ c. butter, softened
- ¾ c. brown sugar, packed
- 1 egg
- ½ tsp. vanilla extract
- 1¼ c. flour
- ½ tsp. baking soda
- ½ tsp. salt
- ½ c. candied red or green maraschino cherries, chopped
- ¼ c. dried apricots, chopped
- ¼ c. raisins
- ¾ c. semi-sweet chocolate chips
- 1 c. nuts, coarsely chopped

Ingredients for filling:

- 2 Tbs. sugar
- 2 Tbs. milk
- 1 Tbs. butter, melted
- 1 egg
- ½ tsp. vanilla extract
- ⅓ c. flour
- ½ tsp. baking soda
- ¼ tsp. salt

Directions:

1. Preheat oven to 350 degrees F.
2. Lightly grease a 9 x 13-inch baking pan.
3. In large bowl, cream butter, brown sugar, egg, and vanilla until creamy.
4. In medium bowl, combine flour, baking soda, and salt; gradually add to butter mixture, blend well.
5. Spread evenly into prepared pan.
6. Bake 12 to 15 minutes, or until lightly browned.
7. Remove from oven, but do not turn oven off.
8. Cool 5 minutes.

9. Meanwhile, prepare vanilla butter filling below.
10. Spread evenly over crust.
11. Sprinkle cherries, apricots, raisins, chocolate chips, and nuts over top.
12. Return to oven; bake 15 minutes until center is set.
13. Cool completely in pan on wire rack; cut into bars.

Directions for filling:

1. In small bowl, beat sugar, milk, butter, egg, and vanilla until smooth.
2. Add flour, baking soda, and salt; beat well.

Christmas Brownies

These brownies are so delicious.

Ingredients:

¾ c. cake flour, sifted
½ tsp. baking powder
¼ tsp. salt
⅓ c. butter
2 sq. unsweetened chocolate, melted
1 c. sugar
2 eggs, well beaten
½ c. walnuts, chopped
1 tsp. vanilla extract

Directions:

1. Preheat oven to 350 degrees F.
2. Lightly grease an 8 x 8-inch square baking pan.
3. Sift flour once and then measure.
4. Add baking powder and salt; sift again.
5. Add butter to chocolate and mix well.
6. In large bowl, add eggs; gradually add sugar beating thoroughly.
7. Stir in chocolate mixture; blend well.
8. Add flour and mix well.
9. Stir in nuts and vanilla.
10. Bake 35 minutes.
11. Cut in squares; remove from pan.
12. Cool on rack.

Fudgey Chocolate Cookie Bars

I am always asked for this delicious recipe by guests I serve them to.

Ingredients:

1¾ c. flour
¾ c. powdered sugar
¼ c. cocoa
1 c. butter, cold
2 c. semi-sweet chocolate chips, divided (12 oz.)
1 can sweetened condensed milk
1 tsp. vanilla extract
1 c. nuts, chopped

Directions:

1. Preheat oven to 350 degrees F.
2. In medium bowl, combine flour, sugar, and cocoa.
3. Cut in butter until crumbly (mixture will be dry).
4. Press firmly on bottom of 9 x 13-inch baking pan.
5. Bake 15 minutes.
6. In medium saucepan, combine 1 cup chocolate chips, milk, and vanilla.
7. Cook over medium heat, stirring constantly, until chips are melted.
8. Pour evenly over prepared crust.
9. Top with nuts and remaining 1 cup chips.
10. Press down firmly.
11. Bake 20 minutes, or until set.
12. Cool in pan on wire rack.
13. Refrigerate, if desired.
14. Cut into bars.
15. Store tightly covered.

Yields: 24 bar cookies.

Mom's Brownies

These are very tasty, frosted brownies.

Ingredients for brownies:

½ c. butter
2 c. sugar
4 eggs, separated, beat whites and save for later
2 sq. chocolate, melted
1½ c. flour, sifted
½ c. milk
1 tsp. vanilla extract
½ c. nuts

Ingredients for frosting:

1 sq. chocolate, melted (2 squares for darker)
¼ c. butter

Directions for brownies:

1. Preheat oven to 325 degrees F.
2. Lightly grease an 8 x 8-inch baking pan.
3. In large bowl, beat butter, sugar, and egg yolks well.
4. Stir in chocolate, then flour and milk; mix well.
5. Fold in egg whites, gently.
6. Bake 30 minutes.

Directions for frosting:

1. In small bowl, mix chocolate and butter.
2. Add sugar and milk to desired thickness.
3. Spread on cooled brownies.

Did You Know? . . . .

Did you know that if you get melted chocolate all over your hands, you're eating it too slowly?

Orange Oatmeal Cookies

My dad always loved oatmeal cookies, and these are flavorful.

Ingredients:

½ c. butter plus ¼ tsp. for the pan
1   egg
¼   c. banana, ripe, mashed (½ banana)
1   tsp. vanilla extract
½   c. brown sugar, packed
1½ tsp. orange zest, grated or minced
1   c. flour, whole wheat
1   tsp. baking powder
1½ c. rolled oats
¾   c. coconut, shredded, unsweetened
1¼ c. walnuts, chopped
½   c. chocolate chips

Directions:

1. Preheat oven to 350 degrees F.
2. Spread ¼ teaspoon of butter on baking sheet.
3. In large bowl, beat butter and egg until well blended and smooth.
4. Gradually beat in banana, vanilla, and sugar.
5. Add orange zest; blend well.
6. In large bowl, combine flour, baking powder, oats, coconut, walnuts, and chocolate chips.
7. Slowly add dry ingredients to wet ingredients and mix thoroughly.
8. Drop by heaping tablespoons of dough 2 inches apart onto baking sheet.
9. Press down lightly.
10. Bake 20 minutes, or until light brown.
11. Cool on wire rack.

Triple Chocolate Oatmeal Cookies

Triple chocolate and double nuts make these oatmeal cookies especially delightful.

Ingredients:

1¾ c. rolled oats, divided
8   Tbs. butter, unsalted, room temperature
½   c. sugar
½   c. brown sugar, firmly packed
1   egg
1   tsp. vanilla extract
1   c. flour
½   tsp. baking powder
½   tsp. baking soda
¼   tsp. salt
½   c. milk chocolate, chopped (3 oz.)
½   c. dark chocolate chips (3 oz.)
½   c. white chocolate, chopped (3 oz.)
½   c. almonds, blanched, chopped
½   c. pecans, chopped

Directions:

1. Preheat oven to 375 degrees F.
2. Place 1½ cup of oats in blender container; process 1 minute until fine.
3. In large bowl, with electric mixer, beat butter with both sugars until smooth.
4. Beat in egg and vanilla.
5. In medium bowl, combine processed oats with flour, baking powder, baking soda, and salt.
6. Slowly add to butter mixture; mix well.
7. Stir in remaining oats, chocolates, almonds, and pecans.
8. Drop by spoonfuls onto ungreased baking sheets.
9. Bake 10 minutes, or until golden brown.
10. Cool slightly on baking sheets before removing.

Chocolate Coconut Macaroons

These are chewy and creamy cookies for everyone to enjoy.

Ingredients

- 2 bars unsweetened baking chocolate (1 oz. ea.)
- 1 can sweetened condensed milk (14 oz.)
- 3 c. sweetened coconut flakes
- 1 tsp. vanilla extract

Directions

1. Preheat oven to 350 degrees F.
2. Generously grease a baking sheet.
3. Melt chocolate in top of double boiler over hot, but not boiling water.
4. In large bowl, stir together chocolate and milk.
5. Add coconut and vanilla; stir until well blended.
6. Drop by teaspoonfuls onto prepared baking sheet.
7. Bake 15 minutes or until set. Do not over bake.
8. Immediately remove from baking sheet to wire rack. Macaroons will stick if allowed to cool on baking sheet.
9. Cool completely before serving.

Yields: 30 cookies.

Did You Know? . . . .

Did you know that apparently people with a sweet tooth live longer? The scientists aren't sure why. It may be that candy is simply more popular among already-healthy people.

Chocolate Delights
A Collection of Chocolate Recipes
Cookbook Delights Series Book 3

Desserts

Table of Contents

Page

Chocolate Apricot Torte

This torte is delicious with apricots.

Ingredients:

1⅓ c. butter
1½ c. plus ⅓ c. sugar, divided
⅔ c. cocoa
5 eggs, separated
2 Tbs. water
1 tsp. vanilla extract
1 c. almonds, blanched, ground
3 Tbs. matzo cake meal
½ c. apricot preserves
chocolate cream frosting (recipe follows)
whole almonds (optional)

Ingredients for chocolate cream frosting

½ c. sugar
¼ c. cocoa
1 c. whipping cream
½ tsp. vanilla extract

Directions:

1. Preheat oven to 350 degrees F.
2. Line bottoms of two 9-inch round baking pans with parchment or wax paper.
3. In medium saucepan, over low heat, melt butter.
4. Add 1½ cups sugar and cocoa; stir until well blended.
5. Remove from heat; cool to room temperature.
6. In large bowl, beat egg yolks until slightly thickened.
7. Gradually add cocoa mixture, beating until blended.
8. Stir in water and vanilla.

9. Stir together ground almonds and cake meal; stir half of mixture into chocolate batter.
10. In small bowl, beat egg whites until foamy.
11. Gradually add remaining sugar, beating until stiff peaks form.
12. Fold remaining almond mixture into beaten whites.
13. Gradually add egg white mixture to chocolate batter, folding gently until well blended.
14. Pour batter into prepared pans.
15. Bake 30 to 35 minutes, or until inserted toothpick in center comes out clean.
16. Cool 10 minutes (cake will settle slightly).
17. Remove from pans to wire racks; peel off paper.
18. Cool completely.
19. Place 1 layer on serving plate.
20. Heat apricot preserves; strain; discard fruit.
21. Spread melted preserves over top of layer.
22. Top with remaining layer.
23. Prepare chocolate cream frosting; spread over top and sides of torte.
24. Refrigerate until serving time.
25. Garnish with whole almonds, if desired.
26. Cover; refrigerate leftover torte.

Directions for chocolate cream frosting:

1. In medium bowl, stir together sugar and cocoa.
2. Add whipping cream and vanilla.
3. Beat until stiff.
4. Makes about 2 cups frosting.

Yields: 12 servings.

Did You Know? . . . .

Did you know that per capita, Americans eat an average of 26.2 pounds of candy each year, split almost equally between candy and chocolate? Chocolate is America's favorite flavor.

Triple Chocolate Torte

This torte is sure to please your chocolate lovers.

Ingredients for torte:

 1½ c. plus 6 Tbs. butter, cut into pieces
 1   c. plus 2 Tbs. cocoa or Dutch processed cocoa
 6   eggs, separated
 2½ c. sugar
 1¼ c. flour
 1   c. almonds, finely chopped
 3   Tbs. amaretto (almond-flavored liqueur) or 1 tsp. almond extract
 2   tsp. vanilla extract

Ingredients for chocolate mousse filling:

 1   pkg. unflavored gelatin
 2   Tbs. water, cold
 ¼   c. water, boiling
 ⅔   c. sugar
 ⅓   c. cocoa or Dutch processed cocoa
 1½ tsp. vanilla extract
 1½ c. whipping cream, cold

Ingredients for ganache glaze:

 ⅓   c. whipping cream
 1   c. semi-sweet chocolate chips

Directions for torte:

1. Preheat oven to 350 degrees F.
2. Grease three 9-inch round baking pans; line bottoms with wax paper and grease paper.
3. In small microwave-safe bowl, place butter.
4. Microwave on high 1 minute until melted; stir in cocoa until smooth.
5. In large bowl, lightly beat egg yolks.

6. Add sugar, and beat until blended.
7. Stir in chocolate mixture; mix well.
8. Stir in flour, almonds, liqueur, and vanilla until blended.
9. In separate bowl, beat egg whites until stiff.
10. Gradually fold into chocolate mixture.
11. Pour into prepared pans.
12. Bake 25 to 30 minutes, or until inserted toothpick in center comes out clean.
13. Cool in pans 10 minutes.
14. Invert onto wire rack; cool completely.
15. Prepare chocolate mousse filling; spread half of mousse on top of each of 2 cake layers, leaving 1 layer plain.
16. Cover; refrigerate until filling is firm.
17. Prepare ganache glaze.
18. On serving plate, stack layers, ending with plain layer.
19. Spread glaze on top; allow to drip down sides.
20. Cover; refrigerate until firm; serve cold.
21. Refrigerate leftover cake.

Directions for chocolate mousse filling:

1. Sprinkle gelatin over cold water in small bowl; stir and let stand 1 minute to soften.
2. Add boiling water; stir until gelatin is completely dissolved (mixture must be clear).
3. In small, cold mixer bowl, stir together sugar and cocoa; add whipping cream and vanilla.
4. Beat until stiff peaks form; pour in gelatin mixture.
5. Beat until well blended

Directions for ganache glaze:

1. Place whipping cream and chocolate chips in small microwave-safe bowl.
2. Microwave on high 30 seconds to 1 minute, until chocolate is melted and mixture is smooth when stirred with wire whisk; cool slightly.

Chocolate Raspberry Cream Crêpes

These chocolate crêpes are excellent with the raspberry cream sauce.

Ingredients for crêpes:

3   eggs
¼ c. sugar
1   c. flour
1   c. milk
1   Tbs. cocoa powder
1   Tbs. butter, melted
1   Tbs. vanilla extract

Ingredients for white sauce:

6   oz. white chocolate baking bar
5   Tbs. whipping cream
2   Tbs. light corn syrup
1½ Tbs. raspberry liqueur
½ tsp. vanilla extract

Ingredients for raspberry cream:

1   c. whipping cream
1   Tbs. raspberry liqueur
1   Tbs. sugar
2   pt. fresh raspberries
    fresh mint sprigs, for garnish

Directions for crêpes:

1. Place all crêpe ingredients in blender or food processor; process until smooth.
2. Heat 6-inch skillet pan over medium heat, coat with canola spray.

3. Pour 2 to 3 tablespoons batter in pan, swirling to form crêpe.
4. Cook 1 minute on each side or until golden.
5. Repeat with remaining batter.
6. Crêpes may be stacked and freeze well.

Directions for white sauce:

1. In small saucepan, over low heat, gently melt chocolate, stirring at intervals; set aside.
2. In another small saucepan, bring cream to boil.
3. Add corn syrup, stirring until blended.
4. Gradually add cream mixture to melted chocolate, stirring until smooth.
5. Stir in liqueur and vanilla.
6. Keep warm.

Directions for raspberry cream:

1. In medium bowl, whip cream, raspberry liqueur, and sugar to form peaks.
2. Fold in ¼ of raspberries.
3. Spoon some chocolate sauce over center of each dessert plate.
4. Spoon a generous 2 tablespoons raspberry cream down center of each crêpe.
5. Fold two sides over and place seam-side down on chocolate sauce.
6. Sprinkle with raspberries and garnish with mint.
7. Serve immediately.

Yields: 14 crêpes.

Did You Know? . . . .

Did you know that a day without chocolate is a day without sunshine?

Chocolate Toffee Crunch Squares

These are so good with chocolate and toffee bits, they disappear fast.

Ingredients:

- 2 pkg. milk chocolate chips (11½ oz. ea.)
- 1 c. English toffee bits or almond toffee bits
- 1 c. salted peanuts
- 1 c. pretzel sticks, halved
- ½ c. sweetened coconut flakes (optional)
- ½ c. white chocolate chips
- 1 tsp. shortening (no substitutions)
- paper candy cups (optional)

Directions:

1. Line a 9-inch square pan with plastic wrap.
2. Place chocolate chips in large microwave-safe bowl and microwave on high for 1 minute; stir.
3. If necessary, microwave on high an additional 15 seconds at a time, stirring after each heating just until chips are melted, and mixture is smooth when stirred.
4. Immediately add toffee bits, peanuts, pretzels, and coconut, if desired; stir to coat.
5. Spread mixture into prepared pan; cover with plastic wrap or foil.
6. Refrigerate 45 minutes or until firm.
7. Place white chips and shortening in small microwave-safe bowl and microwave on high 1 minute; stir.
8. If necessary, microwave on high an additional 15 seconds at a time, stirring after each heating just until chips are melted and mixture is smooth when stirred.
9. Using fork, drizzle white chips mixture over chocolate mixture in pan.

10. Cover and refrigerate 5 minutes or until firm.
11. Bring to room temperature.
12. Remove chocolate mixture from pan and place on cutting board, top side up.
13. Discard plastic wrap.
14. Cut into 1½-inch squares.
15. Place each square in a candy cup, if desired.
16. Store in covered container in a cool place.

Yields: 3 dozen squares.

Chocolate Sticks

Your family will love these "very chocolate" sticks for something a little different from cake or cookies.

Ingredients:

2 eggs, separated
¼ tsp. salt
2 sq. bitter chocolate
½ c. butter
1 c. sugar
½ tsp. vanilla extract
½ c. flour
½ c. pecans or walnuts, chopped

Directions:

1. Preheat oven to 350 degrees F.
2. In small bowl, beat egg whites with salt.
3. In small saucepan, over very low heat, melt chocolate with butter; add sugar and stir well.
4. Stir in eggs, first the yolks and then the whites.
5. Add vanilla and flour; fold in nuts.
6. Bake 20 to 30 minutes, or until inserted toothpick in center comes out clean.
7. Cut into slim, rectangular sticks.

Double Chocolate Cheesecake

Our family loves cheesecake, and this chocolate cheesecake makes a nice variety for a special dessert for those chocolate lovers.

Ingredients for cheesecake:

> 1   c. chocolate wafer crumbs
> ¼   c. butter
> 3   pkg. cream cheese, softened (8 oz. ea.)
> 1¼ c. sugar
> 1   Tbs. flour
> ½   c. Dutch processed cocoa
> 1   c. sour cream
> 1½ tsp. vanilla extract
> ½   tsp. almond extract
> 3   eggs
>   sweetened whipped cream

Directions for cheesecake:

1. Preheat oven to 450 degrees F.
2. In small bowl, combine crumbs and butter; press onto bottom of 9-inch springform pan.
3. In large bowl, with electric mixer on medium speed, combine cream cheese, sugar, and flour; beat until well blended.
4. Beat in cocoa, sour cream, and extracts; blend well.
5. Add eggs, one at a time, beating on low speed just until blended.
6. Pour into crust and bake 10 minutes.
7. Reduce oven temperature to 250 degrees F and continue baking 40 minutes.
8. Remove from oven to wire rack.
9. With knife, loosen cake from side of pan.
10. Cool completely; remove side of pan.
11. Refrigerate several hours before serving.
12. Garnish with whipped cream.
13. Store covered in refrigerator.

Mint Chocolate Chip Ice Cream

Some of my children's favorite ice cream is mint chocolate chip, and we make this homemade ice cream for a special treat.

Ingredients:

1 c. sugar
1 Tbs. cornstarch
4⅔ c. heavy cream
4 lg. egg yolks, beaten lightly
2 Tbs. crème de menthe
2 oz. bittersweet chocolate, fine quality, chopped

Directions:

1. In a saucepan, whisk together sugar and cornstarch.
2. Whisk in milk.
3. Bring mixture to boil over medium heat, stirring frequently; boil 1 minute stirring constantly; remove from heat.
4. In small bowl, stir ¼ cream mixture into yolks; pour into remaining milk mixture, whisking constantly.
5. Cook mixture over low heat, stirring constantly, until slightly thickened, and a thermometer registers 160 degrees F. Do not boil mixture or it will curdle.
6. Stir in crème de menthe and transfer mixture to a bowl.
7. Chill mixture 1 hour, or until cool.
8. Freeze cream mixture in an ice cream maker.
9. During last 15 minutes of freezing time, prepare chocolate.
10. In small heavy saucepan, melt chocolate over low heat, stirring occasionally; cool slightly.
11. Put chocolate in a small sealable plastic bag; seal bag, pressing out excess air.
12. Squeeze chocolate to one corner of bag and snip off ⅛-inch from corner to form a makeshift pastry bag.
13. Add chocolate in a thin stream during last few minutes of freezing time.

White Chocolate Cherry Mousse Cheesecake

This is an absolutely heavenly dessert, sure to impress your loved ones on any day of the year. The red cherries and white chocolate are beautiful on a special occasion table, like Christmas and Valentine's Day celebrations.

Ingredients:

- 9 oz. white chocolate
- 3 tsp. gelatin powder
- 1 oz. water, warm
- 4 c. whipped cream, sweetened
- 1 c. sugar
- 4 c. cream cheese, softened
- ½ c. graham cracker crumbs
- ½ c. shortbread-type cookies, crumbled
- ½ c. pecans, chopped
- ½ c. caramel fudge sauce (recipe on page 179)
- ¼ c. sun-dried cherries
- 2 Tbs. butter, melted
- 2 oz. whole pecans, for garnish
- 2 Tbs. caramel fudge sauce, for garnish
- 2 Tbs. dried cherries, chopped for garnish

Directions:

1. In small saucepan, over low heat, melt chocolate.
2. In small cup, soften gelatin in water.
3. Using electric mixer on medium speed, beat cream cheese and sugar until light and fluffy.
4. Add melted white chocolate and softened gelatin.
5. Continue mixing for 2 minutes.
6. Fold in whipped cream and sun-dried cherries.
7. To assemble, grease a 10-inch mold with butter and cover sides with shortbread crumbs.

8. Spread graham cracker crumbs on bottom, then drizzle caramel sauce over the crumbs.
9. Pour half the cheesecake mixture over first drizzled layer of crumbs; top with chopped pecans.
10. Cover with remainder of cheesecake mixture.
11. Decorate top with whole pecans and sun-dried cherries.
12. Drizzle whole cheesecake with caramel topping.
13. Refrigerate until cake is firm.

Chocolate Dessert Cups

You will be delighted with these edible dessert cups, which can be used to serve ice cream, pudding, fresh fruit, and more. You can make them a week in advance, then refrigerate in an airtight container.

Ingredients:

6 sq. semi-sweet chocolate (1 oz.)
1 tsp. shortening (no substitutions)

Directions:

1. Cut out four 6-inch circles from wax paper; place on a baking sheet.
2. In microwave, melt chocolate and shortening; stir until smooth.
3. Pour 2 tablespoons melted chocolate into the center of each circle.
4. Spread chocolate to within 1 inch of edge.
5. Refrigerate for 3 to 4 minutes, or until chocolate does not spread when handled.
6. Drape circles, wax paper side down, over inverted 6-ounce custard cups or small bowls.
7. Shape edges if desired; chill 10 minutes.
8. Carefully peel wax paper from chocolate.

Chocolate Pudding

*Chocolate pudding is always a favorite comfort food.
Try this delicious recipe.*

Ingredients:

- ¼ c. cornstarch
- ½ c. sugar
- ⅛ tsp. salt
- 3 c. whole milk
- 6 oz. semi-sweet chocolate, good quality, coarsely chopped
- 1 tsp. pure vanilla extract

Directions:

1. In top of double boiler, combine cornstarch, sugar, and salt.
2. Slowly whisk in milk, scraping bottom and sides or pan incorporate dry ingredients.
3. Place over gently simmering water, stir occasionally, scraping bottom and sides; using a whisk as necessary should lumps begin to form.
4. After 15 to 20 minutes, when mixture begins to thicken and coats the back of the spoon, add the chocolate.
5. Continue stirring 2 to 4 minutes, or until pudding is smooth and thickened; remove from heat.
6. Stir in vanilla.
7. Strain through a fine-mesh strainer, (to make sure there are no lumps), into a serving bowl or into a large measuring cup with a spout and pour into individual serving dishes.
8. Note: If you like pudding skin, pull plastic wrap over the top of the serving dish or dishes before refrigerating.
9. If you dislike pudding skin, place plastic wrap on top of the pudding and smooth it gently against the surface before refrigerating.
10. Refrigerate at least 30 minutes and up to 3 days.

Chocolate Delights
A Collection of Chocolate Recipes
Cookbook Delights Series Book 3

Dressings, Sauces, and Condiments

Table of Contents

Page

Chocolate Almond Butter

Your family will enjoy this chocolate almond butter.

Ingredients:

> ¼ c. honey
> ½ c. almond paste
> ¼ c. butter, softened
> ¼ c. semi-sweet chocolate, melted

Directions:

1. Gently melt chocolate over a double boiler or in a microwave.
2. In small bowl, with electric mixer, blend honey, chocolate, and almond paste together.
3. Beat in butter until creamy.
4. Serve with warm muffins or English muffins.

Chocolate Cashew Butter

This cashew butter with chocolate is delicious, and so simple to make.

Ingredients:

> 2 c. cashews, unsalted, roasted
> 2 Tbs. canola oil
> ¼ tsp. salt
> 1 tsp. sugar (optional)
> ¼ c. sweetened baking cocoa
> canola oil, as needed

Directions:

1. In food processor or blender, combine nuts, oil, salt, sugar, and cocoa.
2. Process on high speed for 30 seconds.

3. Scrape down sides with a rubber spatula; process to desired smoothness, adding more oil, 1 teaspoon at a time, if a smoother butter is desired.
4. Adjust seasoning, to taste.
5. Place in airtight container; refrigerate until ready to use.

Espresso Hot Fudge Sauce

If you like espresso and chocolate, you will enjoy this wonderful sauce.

Ingredients:

⅓ c. freshly brewed strong coffee
⅓ c. brown sugar
½ c. Dutch process cocoa
1 pinch salt
2 Tbs. butter, in small pieces
3 Tbs. heavy cream
1 tsp. instant espresso powder

Directions:

1. In small saucepan, over medium heat, combine coffee and brown sugar.
2. Cook, stirring frequently, until sugar is melted.
3. Add cocoa and salt; whisk until smooth.
4. Reduce heat to low; whisk in butter and cream.
5. Whisk in instant espresso; stir until dissolved.
6. Serve over ice cream.
7. Note: This sauce may be refrigerated up to 2 weeks.
8. Reheat in heavy pan over low heat, stirring frequently.

Yields: ¾ cup.

Shortcut Chocolate Sauce

This is a quick recipe for chocolate sauce for desserts or ice cream.

Ingredients:

> 1 c. semi-sweet chocolate chips
> ¾ c. whipping cream
> 1 tsp. vanilla extract

Directions:

1. In small saucepan, over low heat, heat chocolate chips and whipping cream, stirring constantly.
2. Continue to cook, stirring constantly, until chocolate is melted and sauce is smooth.
3. Stir in vanilla and serve over dessert or ice cream.

Yields: 1¼ cups.

Chocolate Cream Sauce

This is excellent with heavy whipping cream.

Ingredients:

> 1 pkg. semi-sweet or bittersweet chocolate, cut into small pieces (12 oz.)
> 1 c. heavy whipping cream
> ⅓ c. sugar
> ⅓ c. light corn syrup
> 1½ tsp. pure vanilla extract
> 1 Tbs. strong liquor, such as rum, or liqueurs such as Grand Marnier or brandy (optional)

Directions:

1. Place chopped chocolate in medium-size stainless steel bowl and set aside.

2. In small saucepan, over low heat, combine cream, sugar, and corn syrup.
3. Bring to a boil, stirring often.
4. Remove from heat.
5. Pour immediately over the chocolate.
6. Let stand until chocolate has melted, then stir until smooth.
7. Stir in vanilla extract and liquor.
8. Store sauce in refrigerator in a tightly covered container for up to 2 weeks.
9. Reheat over simmering water before serving, if desired.

Yields: 2 cups.

Caramel Fudge Sauce

This recipe will leave you grinning. I love caramel with chocolate, and this is no exception.

Ingredients:

½   c. brown sugar, packed
1½ c. sugar
¾   c. cocoa
¼   c. flour
½   tsp. salt
1   can evaporated milk (14 oz.)
1   c. water
2   Tbs. butter
2   tsp. vanilla extract

Directions:

1. In small saucepan, combine sugar, cocoa, flour, and salt; add milk, water, and butter.
2. Cook over medium heat, stirring constantly, until boiling.
3. Cook 5 minutes longer.
4. Remove from heat; cool.
5. Stir in vanilla.

5-Minute Chocolate Sauce

This makes an easy and fast chocolate sauce, but not at the expense of losing the wonderful flavor.

Ingredients:

> 1 c. semi-sweet chocolate, coarsely chopped
> ¾ c. light cream
> 2 Tbs. butter, unsalted, cut into small pieces

Directions:

1. In medium saucepan, over very low heat, warm cream and chocolate, 5 or 6 minutes, stirring occasionally until smooth.
2. When completely melted, remove from heat.
3. Whisk in butter.
4. Mix in any of the optional flavorings listed below, and serve.
5. Store the sauce in a clean, tightly covered jar.
6. Reheat the sauce right in the jar, in a saucepan of hot water, with the lid loosened.
7. This will last about 2 weeks refrigerated.

Additional ingredients for chocolate mint sauce:

> 2 Tbs. white crème de menthe

Directions for chocolate mint sauce:

1. Whisk 2 tablespoons white crème de menthe into sauce with the butter.

Additional ingredients for mocha sauce variation:

> 2 Tbs. instant coffee powder
> 2 Tbs. coffee liqueur or any other liqueur or flavoring

Directions for mocha sauce:

1. Heat cream first; whisk in instant coffee.
2. Add chocolate and proceed as above.
3. When sauce is removed from heat, whisk in butter and 2 tablespoons coffee liqueur.

Yields: 2 cups.

Chocolate Orange Sauce

For those who get bored with chocolate sauce, you will enjoy this one with the orange flavor.

Ingredients:

⅓ c. sugar
⅓ c. unsweetened cocoa powder
¼ c. water
2 Tbs. orange liqueur or orange juice
¼ c. light corn syrup
1 tsp. vanilla extract

Directions:

1. In small saucepan, combine sugar and cocoa; stir well.
2. Add water, stirring until smooth.
3. Add liqueur or orange juice and corn syrup; stir well.
4. Place over medium heat; bring to boil, stirring constantly.
5. Remove from heat.
6. Stir in vanilla.
7. Pour into a bowl.
8. Cover; chill until ready to serve.

Yields: 14 servings.

Luscious Chocolate Butter

You will enjoy this simple chocolate butter.

Ingredients:

½ c. butter, softened
¼ c. semi-sweet chocolate chips, melted, cooled

Directions:

1. Cut butter into chunks and place in food processor or blender.
2. Add melted chocolate chips as well.
3. Process 30 seconds, until smooth.
4. Place mixture in a small container; cover.
5. Refrigerate until ready to use.
6. Bring back to room temperature before serving.

Coconut Fudge Sauce

This is a delicious fudge sauce to serve over ice cream.

Ingredients:

¾ c. evaporated milk
½ c. sugar
1½ tsp. butter
2 tsp. coconut extract
1 pkg. semi-sweet chocolate chips (6 oz.)

Directions:

1. In large saucepan, over medium heat, add milk, chocolate chips, and sugar.
2. Stir constantly until chocolate is melted and mixture begins to boil.

3. Remove from heat; stir in butter and extract.
4. Pour into jars; cover tightly.
5. Serve warm or cold over ice cream.
6. Note: Refrigerate no longer than 4 weeks.

Cousins Hot Fudge Sauce

This recipe is so quick and easy to remember, and the best hot fudge sauce I ever tasted – bar none.

Ingredients:

    1 c. sugar
    ¼ c. cocoa
    ¼ c. milk
    ¼ c. butter
    1 Tbs. light corn syrup
    ¼ tsp. vanilla extract
      dash of salt

Directions:

1. In small saucepan, combine all ingredients except vanilla.
2. Boil 2 minutes.
3. Remove from heat.
4. Stir in vanilla.

Variations:

1. For cooled topping, add a splash of milk.
2. Place pan in sink of cold water.
3. If not using immediately, stir in splash of milk anyway, or it will sugar.
4. For darker chocolate, add less sugar or more cocoa.
5. For thinner topping, add a bit more milk.

Sloppy Dawg Sauce

This is a great sauce to serve warm as a topping for grilled hot dogs, burgers, chicken or steak.

Ingredients:

>
> 3 Tbs. butter
> 1 c. onion, finely chopped
> ¾ c. ketchup
> ¼ c. brown sugar, packed
> 3 Tbs. cocoa
> 3 Tbs. steak sauce
> 1 Tbs. tomato paste
> 1 Tbs. white vinegar
> ¼ tsp. dry mustard
> ¼ tsp. hot pepper sauce

Directions:

1. In medium saucepan, over medium heat, melt butter; add onion; cook until tender.
2. Stir in remaining ingredients; bring to boil, stirring occasionally.
3. Remove from heat.
4. If sauce is too thick, add water 1 tablespoon at a time.
5. Refrigerate leftovers.

Chocolate Cherry Chutney

This chunky, chocolaty treat is delicious served over pound cake, ice cream or other desserts, and is great to give as a gift.

Ingredients:

>
> 2 jars maraschino cherries (16 oz. ea.)
> 1 c. semi-sweet chocolate, coarsely chopped
> 1 can evaporated milk (5 oz.)
> 1 cup powdered sugar
> 1½ c. almonds, slivered, chopped, toasted

1   c. white chocolate chips

Directions:

1. Drain cherries, reserving ¼ cup juice; set aside.
2. Chop cherries.
3. In large microwavable bowl, combine chocolate and milk.
4. Microwave on high 3 to 4 minutes or until melted, stirring after 2 minutes.
5. Add powdered sugar and reserved cherry juice.
6. Microwave 1 minute; stir until smooth.
7. Stir in cherries, toasted almonds, and white chocolate chips.
8. Spoon into 4 food-safe containers.
9. Store refrigerated up to 4 weeks.

Yields: 4 (1¼-cup) containers.

Rustic Spice Seasoning

This is a great seasoning or dry rub for poultry, pork, beef, seafood, salads, soups or vegetables.

Ingredients:

8   Tbs. paprika
½   tsp. cayenne pepper
5   Tbs. black pepper
6   Tbs. onion powder
3   Tbs. salt
2½ Tbs. dried oregano
2½ Tbs. dried thyme
3   Tbs. toffee bits, crushed
3   Tbs. cocoa

Directions:

1. In medium bowl, combine all ingredients.
2. Store in airtight container in cool, dry place for up to 6 weeks.

Sambuca Chocolate Sauce

Sambuca adds a distinctively different twist to this chocolate sauce.

Ingredients:

½ c. water
⅔ c. sugar
¾ c. unsweetened Dutch process cocoa
½ tsp. salt
½ c. heavy cream
¼ c. butter, unsalted
1 tsp. vanilla extract
¼ c. sambuca, or to taste

Directions:

1. In small, heavy saucepan, combine water and sugar; bring to boil, stirring until sugar is dissolved.
2. Remove from heat; whisk in cocoa until smooth.
3. Whisk in salt, cream, and butter; return pan to moderately low heat, whisking until butter is melted.
4. Simmer sauce 2 minutes, until thickened slightly; stir in vanilla and sambuca.
5. Cool sauce completely.
6. Transfer to a jar with a tight-fitting lid.
7. Sauce keeps covered and chilled for 1 month.
8. Serve sauce warm (optional) over ice cream.

Yields: 2 cups

Did You Know? . . . .

Did you know that money talks? But chocolate sings.

Chocolate Delights
A Collection of Chocolate Recipes
Cookbook Delights Series Book 3

Jams, Jellies, and Syrups

Table of Contents

Page

A Basic Guide for Canning Jams, Jellies, and Syrups

1. Wash jars in hot, soapy water inside and out with brush or soft cloth.
2. Run your finger around rim of each jar, discarding any with cracks or chips.
3. Rinse well in clean, clear, hot water, using tongs to avoid burns to hands or fingers.
4. Place upside down on clean cloth to drain well.
5. Place lids in boiling water for 2 minutes to sterilize and keep hot until placing on rim of jar.
6. Immediately prior to filling each jar, immerse in very hot water with tongs to heat jar (avoids breakage of jar with hot liquid).
7. Fill jar to within 1 inch of top of rim or to level recommended in recipe.
8. Wipe rim with clean damp cloth to remove any particles of food, and check again for any chips or cracks.
9. With tongs, place lid from hot bath directly onto rim of jar.
10. Using gloves, cloth, or holders, tighten lid firmly onto jar with ring or use single formed lid in place of ring to cover inner lid. Do not tighten down too hard as it may impede sealing.
11. Place on protected surface to cool, taking care to not disturb lid and ring. A slight indentation of lid will be apparent when sealed.
12. Leave overnight until thoroughly cooled.
13. When cooled, wipe jars with damp cloth and then label and date each.
14. Store upright on shelf in cool, dark place.

Did You Know? . . . .

Did you know that if you put "eat chocolate" at the top of your list of things to do, you'll already have one thing done?

Chocolate Blackberry Jam

The blackberries combined with a touch of chocolate make a refreshing new flavor.

Ingredients:

    7 pt. blackberries, fresh or frozen
    3 sq. unsweetened chocolate
    4 c. sugar
    1 box fruit pectin
    ½ tsp. butter

Directions:

1. Crush berries thoroughly, 1 cup at a time.
2. If using frozen berries, use both liquid and solids. Sieve half of the pulp to remove some seeds if desired. Removing seeds causes waste, so be sure you have enough berries.
3. Measure 6 cups of crushed fruit into 6 or 8-quart heavy saucepan.
4. Break chocolate squares into smaller pieces and add them to saucepan.
5. Measure sugar into separate bowl.
6. Mix ¼ cup sugar from measured amount with pectin in small bowl.
7. Stir pectin-sugar mixture into fruit in saucepan.
8. Add butter.
9. Bring quickly to full rolling boil and boil exactly 1 minute, stirring constantly.
10. Remove from heat.
11. Skim foam, and ladle into pint or half-pint jars.
12. Process following the canning guide on page 188.

Did You Know? . . . .

Did you know that chocolate is cheaper than therapy? And you don't need an appointment!

Blueberry Syrup

This delicious syrup may be used for Chocoberry Milk Chiller on page 60, or try it on other chocolate recipes for a delicious chocolate-blueberry combination.

Ingredients:

1 c. blueberries, fresh or frozen, thawed
¾ c. sugar
⅓ c. water
2 tsp. fresh lemon juice

Directions:

1. In saucepan, combine all ingredients; bring to boil.
2. Reduce heat; simmer until thickened to desired consistency.
3. Remove from heat; cool to room temperature before serving.
4. If thinner syrup is desired, strain through a fine mesh strainer while still hot.

Yields: 1 cup.

Chocolate Peppermint Syrup

This delicious chocolate peppermint syrup may be served over many different items. Enjoy!

Ingredients:

¼ c. butter
2 sq. unsweetened chocolate (1 oz.)
1⅓ c. sugar
⅛ tsp. salt
⅔ c. light cream
½ tsp. vanilla extract
½ c. whipped cream

½ c. peppermint candy, coarsely chopped

Directions:

1. In heavy saucepan, over low heat, melt butter and chocolate. Stir occasionally.
2. Remove from heat; stir in sugar and salt gradually, mix until well combined.
3. Gradually stir in cream and vanilla; return to heat.
4. Over low heat, cook 5 minutes, until sugar is dissolved; cool.
5. Stir in whipped cream and candy.
6. Refrigerate.

Yields: 3 cups.

Chocolate Syrup

This syrup is quick and easy to make, and very good.

Ingredients:

1 c. cocoa
2 c. sugar
¼ tsp. salt
1 c. water
1 Tbs. vanilla extract

Directions:

1. In small saucepan, combine cocoa and sugar; blend until smooth.
2. Add water and salt; mix well.
3. Over medium heat, bring mixture to boil.
4. Boil until thick, stirring constantly.
5. Remove from heat; cool.
6. Stir in vanilla.

Yields: 1 pint.

Chocolate Cranberry Jam

This chocolate cranberry jam is delightful with poultry or lamb. Spread on toast, biscuits, or scones for a luscious breakfast.

Ingredients:

> 1 bag fresh cranberries (12 oz.)
> 1½ c. sugar
> ⅓ c. water
> 1 star anise
> 2 tsp. orange zest
> 2½ oz. bittersweet chocolate, finely chopped

Directions:

1. In large, nonreactive saucepan, combine sugar and water. Mix until sugar is completely covered with water, resembling wet sand.
2. Add star anise and orange zest.
3. Wet your hand or a pastry brush and run it around the edge of the pot to remove any stray sugar crystals.
4. Place pan over medium heat.
5. Bring sugar mixture to simmer.
6. Continue to simmer briskly, without stirring, until sugar reaches hardball stage (248 degrees F.) and the bubbles on the surface begin to look evenly sized.
7. Immediately add cranberries, stirring with a rubber spatula.
8. Reduce heat to medium-low.
9. Continue to cook, stirring often, until cranberries have softened and the jam thickly coats the back of a spoon.
10. Remove from heat.

11. Immediately stir in chocolate until completely combined.
12. Transfer to jar(s) to cool.
13. Store in refrigerator.
14. Note: When you add the cranberries, they may begin to clump together. They will begin to pop as their skins burst, releasing their juices and melt the sugar again.

Gooey Chocolate Jam

This chocolate jam is wonderful on French toast and waffles.

Ingredients:

    2 Tbs. baking cocoa
    2 Tbs. sugar
    1 Tbs. flour
    1 c. milk, or more
    1 tsp. vanilla extract

Directions:

1. In heavy saucepan, combine cocoa, sugar, and flour; mix thoroughly.
2. Add milk, a little at a time, mixing until smooth (mixture should be of "spreading" consistency).
3. Place over medium heat; bring to simmer, stirring frequently, until thickened.
4. Check for desired thickness and sweetness; adjust if necessary.
5. Remove from heat; stir in vanilla.
6. Pour over buttered biscuits, and serve with cold milk.

Yields: 2 servings.

Chocolate Peach Jam

Try this unique flavored jam on your toast, bagels, or English muffins.

Ingredients:

  11 lb. peaches
  1   c. white or dark chocolate, chopped

Directions:

  1. Preheat oven to 350 degrees F.
  2. Wash peaches, divide into halves, remove pits.
  3. Place in appropriate sized baking dish.
  4. Bake 3 hours, or until peaches fall apart and thicken (take them out from oven periodically to stir them). Peach jam is done when wooden spoon leaves clean tracks in the bottom of dish while you mix it.
  5. Remove jam from oven.
  6. Stir chocolate into hot jam; mix until chocolate is melted.
  7. Pour into sterilized, warm jam jars; seal.
  8. Cover jars with a blanket to cool gradually overnight.
  9. Store in cold place.

Chocolate Praline Syrup

This syrup is delicious over waffles or ice cream. We have also poured it on pies and cakes.

Ingredients:

  1 c. whipping cream
  ⅔ c. brown sugar, packed
  ⅔ c. butter
  1 c. semi-sweet chocolate chips

1 c. pecans, chopped
ice cream

Directions:

1. In medium saucepan, over medium heat, bring cream, brown sugar, and butter to boil, stirring constantly.
2. Reduce heat; simmer 2 minutes stirring occasionally.
3. Remove from heat.
4. Stir in chocolate chips until melted and smooth.
5. Stir in pecans.
6. Serve warm over ice cream.
7. Store in refrigerator.

Chocolate Raspberry Jam

Chocolate and raspberry together is always a delicious combination.

Ingredients:

4½ c. fresh raspberries
3   c. sugar
¼ c. semi-sweet chocolate, melted

Directions:

1. In top of double boiler, gently melt chocolate.
2. Place all ingredients in heavy saucepan over medium heat.
3. Bring to boil, stirring occasionally.
4. Increase heat to high; cook 20 minutes, stirring constantly. As mixture begins to thicken, watch carefully to prevent sticking.
5. When mixture is of jam-like consistency, remove from heat.
6. Process following the canning guide on page 188.

Chocolate Strawberry Jam

You will enjoy this delicious chocolate strawberry jam.

Ingredients:

    7 pt. fresh strawberries
    3 sq. unsweetened chocolate, chopped into pieces
    4 c. sugar
    1 box fruit pectin
    ½ tsp. butter

Directions:

1. In blender, crush berries thoroughly, 1 cup at a time. If using frozen berries, use both liquid and solids.
2. Sieve half of pulp to remove some seeds if desired. Removing seeds causes waste, so be sure you have enough berries.
3. Measure 6 cups of crushed fruit into 6 or 8-quart heavy saucepan.
4. Add chocolate pieces.
5. Measure sugar into separate bowl. Take ¼ cup of sugar out of bowl, and mix with pectin in another small bowl.
6. Stir pectin mixture into fruit mixture; add butter.
7. Bring quickly to full rolling boil; boil 1 minute, stirring constantly.
8. Remove from heat.
9. Skim foam and ladle into pint or half-pint jars.
10. Process following the canning guide on page 188.

Pear and Chocolate Jam

Try this different flavor combination on your toast, or bagel.

Ingredients:

    1 lemon, juiced

2 lb. pears, peeled, cored, diced
3 c. sugar
⅓ lb. bittersweet chocolate, chopped (1 c.)

Directions:

1. Place a small plate in your freezer.
2. In large bowl, add lemon juice and pears; mix well.
3. In large saucepan, over medium-high heat, combine pears with sugar; bring to boil.
4. Cook 20 to 30 minutes, stirring occasionally. Skim foam if necessary.
5. Pour a little jam on your cold plate.
6. Wait a few seconds. If it doesn't run, it is set, otherwise, keep cooking and try again a few minutes later.
7. Stir chocolate into jam; bring to simmer.
8. Remove from heat.
9. Process following the canning guide on page 188.

Chocolate Maple Syrup

This syrup is best served warm over ice cream, favorite dessert, pancakes, or waffles.

Ingredients:

1½ c. pure maple syrup
3 Tbs. unsweetened cocoa powder, sifted
¼ c. butter
⅛ tsp. salt

Directions:

1. In heavy saucepan, over medium heat, heat maple syrup until hot.
2. Whisk in cocoa, butter, and salt.
3. Whisk 1 minute until combined.
4. Serve warm.
5. Store in refrigerator up to 7 days.

Chocolate Caramel Syrup

This is a delicious syrup that can be used to make a latté. It is also good served over ice cream or your favorite cake or dessert.

Ingredients:

    1 c. heavy cream
    1 c. light corn syrup
    ½ c. sugar
    ½ c. brown sugar, packed
    ⅛ tsp. salt
    1 c. milk chocolate, chopped (8 oz.)
    ¼ c. butter

Directions:

1. In medium saucepan, combine cream, corn syrup, sugars, and salt.
2. Over medium-high heat, bring to rolling boil.
3. Boil 8 to 10 minutes until thick and deep brown.
4. Remove from heat.
5. Stir in chocolate and butter until smooth.
6. Note: To make a latté, mix 2 tablespoons syrup with espresso in coffee mug.
7. Pour in 1 cup steamed milk; stir, lifting from the bottom of mug, until blended.
8. Top with whipped cream and chocolate shavings.
9. Place syrup in squeeze bottle, and keep in refrigerator. Warm in microwave before using.

Did You Know? . . . .

Did you know that there is nothing better than a good friend, except a good friend with chocolate?

Chocolate Delights
A Collection of Chocolate Recipes
Cookbook Delights Series Book 3

Main Dishes

Table of Contents

Page

Chicken Enchiladas

I love enchiladas and these have a surprising twist. The dark chocolate actually adds flavor to the savory enchilada sauce. Again, the secret is to allow the flavors to blend.

Ingredients for chocolate enchilada sauce:

 1 Tbs. canola oil
 2 garlic cloves, minced
 1 tsp. onion, minced
 ½ tsp. dried oregano
 2½ tsp. chili powder
 ½ tsp. dried basil
 ¼ tsp. ground black pepper
 ¼ tsp. salt
 ¼ tsp. ground cumin
 1 tsp. dried parsley
 ¼ c. salsa
 ¾ c. tomato sauce
 ½ c. dark or semi-sweet chocolate chips
 1½ c. water

Ingredients for enchiladas:

 4 Tbs. canola oil
 2 lb. skinless boneless chicken breasts, cut into strips
 1 med. yellow onion, diced
 2 Tbs. garlic, chopped
 1 tsp. salt
 ¼ tsp. ground black pepper
 1 Tbs. ground chili powder
 1 Tbs. light brown sugar
 1 bunch cilantro leaves, chopped
 ½ c. chicken broth
 5 c. Cheddar cheese, shredded, divided
 20 corn tortillas

Directions for enchiladas:

1. Preheat oven to 375 degrees F.
2. Lightly grease two 9 x 13-inch baking pans.
3. Prepare chocolate enchilada sauce; set aside.
4. In large, heavy skillet, heat oil over medium-high heat (almost smoking).
5. Carefully add chicken, onion, garlic, salt, pepper; cook until brown, stirring occasionally.
6. Add chili powder, brown sugar, and cilantro.
7. Deglaze this with chicken broth.
8. Remove from heat; cool.
9. Pull chicken apart by hand into shredded strips.
10. Stir in 3 cups cheese.
11. Wrap corn tortillas in damp cloth; microwave on high for 10 to 20 seconds until soft and pliable.
12. Spoon ⅓ cup chicken mixture into center of tortilla and roll.
13. Place rolled enchiladas (seam side down) into prepared baking pan.
14. Pour chocolate enchilada sauce over enchiladas.
15. Sprinkle with remaining 2 cups cheese; cover.
16. Bake 20 minutes; garnish as desired.

Directions for chocolate enchilada sauce:

1. In large saucepan, heat oil over medium heat.
2. Add garlic; sauté for 1 to 2 minutes.
3. Stir in onion, oregano, chili powder, basil, pepper, salt, cumin, parsley, salsa, tomato sauce, chocolate chips, and water; heat to boiling.
4. Reduce heat to low; simmer for 15 to 20 minutes.

Yields: 2½ cups sauce.

Did You Know? . . . .

Did you know that if God had meant us to be thin, He would not have created chocolate?

Chicken Mole over Rice

I was introduced to mole sauce as an adult, and I find it very flavorful. I always liked chocolate as a dessert, and now I find that chocolate is also great when used as a subtle flavoring in a main dish. Try this chicken mole over rice; it is very good.

Ingredients:

2¼ c. water
1   c. rice
½   tsp. salt, divided
2   tsp. olive oil, organic extra virgin
1   lb. skinless boneless chicken breasts
1   lg. red onion, halved, thinly sliced
4   garlic cloves, finely chopped
2   green bell peppers, cut into thin strips
1½ c. canned tomatoes, crushed
⅔   c. water
1   Tbs. unsweetened cocoa powder
2   tsp. brown sugar, packed
2   tsp. organic red wine vinegar
½   tsp. cinnamon

Directions:

1. In medium saucepan, bring water to boil.
2. Add rice and ¼ teaspoon salt.
3. Reduce heat to low; cover.
4. Simmer, 17 minutes, or until rice is tender.
5. In large skillet, heat oil over medium heat.
6. Add chicken; cook 2 minutes per side until golden.
7. Remove with a slotted spoon.
8. Add onion and garlic; cook 7 minutes, stirring frequently, until onion is tender.
9. Add peppers and cook 5 minutes, or until softened.
10. Stir in remaining salt, tomatoes, water, cocoa powder, brown sugar, vinegar, and cinnamon.
11. Bring to boil, add chicken; reduce heat.
12. Cover; simmer 10 minutes.

13. Uncover, cook 3 to 5 minutes, stirring occasionally, until chicken is cooked through and sauce is slightly thickened.
14. Transfer chicken to a cutting board, thinly slice, and spoon chicken and sauce over rice.

Yields: 4 servings.

Rosemary Beef Medallions

My daughter loves rosemary, and the combination of rosemary with cocoa powder is very flavorful indeed. Do try these rosemary beef medallions.

Ingredients:

1 lb. beef tenderloin
2 Tbs. butter, divided
½ tsp. cocoa powder
⅛ tsp. salt
1 garlic clove, finely chopped
¼ tsp. dried rosemary leaves
¼ c. dry red wine or beef broth

Directions:

1. Cut beef into ¾-inch slices.
2. In large skillet, over medium-high heat, melt 1 tablespoon butter.
3. Sauté beef 4 to 5 minutes on each side, turning once, until brown; center should be medium rare.
4. Remove beef to warm platter; keep warm.
5. Cook and stir remaining butter, cocoa powder, salt, garlic, and rosemary in skillet until bubbly.
6. Gradually stir in wine; bring to boil.
7. Boil and stir 1 minute.
8. Serve over beef.

Chicken Olé Mole

The secret to making good mole is to make sure you slow-cook the sauce and blend the flavors so that all the fragrances blend. This is very easy to make and actually quite good.

Ingredients:

2 Tbs. olive oil, divided
1 chicken, cut into pieces (2-3 lb.)
½ c. onion, finely chopped
½ c. green pepper, finely chopped
1 sm. garlic clove, minced
⅓ c. almonds, slivered
⅓ c. raisins
1½ Tbs. sesame seeds, toasted
½-1 c. chicken broth
1 can tomato sauce (8 oz.)
2 oz. unsweetened chocolate
1 tsp. hot sauce
½ tsp. ground cinnamon
¼ tsp. ground allspice

Directions:

1. In large skillet, over medium-high heat, heat 1 tablespoon oil.
2. Add chicken; cook 10 minutes, or until browned on all sides.
3. Remove chicken and set aside.
4. Add remaining oil to skillet; add onion, green pepper, and garlic.
5. Cook 3 to 5 minutes, stirring often.
6. Remove from heat.
7. Place almonds, raisins, and sesame seeds in food processor or blender; process until a paste forms.

8. Add mixture to vegetables in skillet along with ½ cup broth, tomato sauce, chocolate, hot sauce, cinnamon, and allspice.
9. Over medium heat, cook and stir for 2 to 3 minutes until chocolate melts.
10. Return chicken to skillet, coating pieces well with sauce.
11. If sauce is too thick, add a little more broth.
12. Reduce heat to low.
13. Cover; simmer 30 to 40 minutes until chicken is tender, and no longer pink.

Yields: 4 servings.

Beef Curry

This beef is delicious with the flavoring combination. I am sure you will enjoy this new taste for beef.

Ingredients:

    1 lb. stew beef, cubed
    3 Tbs. olive oil
    2 Tbs. curry powder
    1 oz. unsweetened chocolate
    ¼ c. molasses
    ¼ c. tomato sauce
    1 qt. orange juice
       salt and pepper, to taste

Directions:

1. In large skillet, brown meat in oil.
2. When meat is lightly browned, add curry and continue browning.
3. Add remaining ingredients and bring to boil.
4. Simmer 1 hour, continuing to add juice as needed.

Easy Chicken Mole

This recipe offers a similar taste to a classic mole sauce. It does not have the depth of flavor of a traditional mole, but it does not take hours to prepare, nor use hard-to-find ingredients.

Ingredients:

> 1 Tbs. canola oil
> ½ c. onion, minced
> 4 garlic cloves, minced
> 6 chicken breast halves, boneless, skinless
> 2 c. tomato purée (16 oz.)
> ½ c. salsa
> ½ c. almonds, ground
> 2 Tbs. sesame seeds, crushed
> 4 tsp. unsweetened cocoa
> 1 tsp. cumin
> 1 tsp. Mexican oregano
> ½ tsp. nutmeg
> ½ tsp. allspice
> salt, to taste
> pepper, freshly ground, to taste

Directions:

1. Heat oil in a large, heavy skillet.
2. Add onion and sauté 4 minutes.
3. Add garlic and chicken.
4. Sauté chicken for 2 minutes on each side, or until lightly browned.
5. Add remaining ingredients.
6. Bring to boil; reduce heat and simmer 10 minutes.
7. Continue to cook sauce until chicken is cooked through.
8. Once chicken is thoroughly cooked, remove from sauce and place on a warm platter.

9. Continue to cook sauce a few minutes more until it has thickened.
10. Serve hot over the chicken with rice.

Yields: 6 servings.

Savory Chili with Pasta

Cocoa adds a warm flavor to this chili with pasta. Enjoy!

Ingredients:

2   c. rotelle or rotini pasta, uncooked (6 oz.)
1   lb. ground beef
1   c. onion, chopped
2   cans tomato sauce (15 oz. ea.)
2   cans red kidney beans, undrained (15 oz. ea.)
3   Tbs. cocoa
2¼ tsp. chili powder
¾   tsp. ground black pepper
½   tsp. salt
    Parmesan cheese, grated

Directions:

1. Cook pasta according to package directions; drain.
2. In large skillet, cook ground beef and onion until meat is thoroughly done, and onion is tender. If necessary, drain fat.
3. Stir in soup, kidney beans, cocoa, chili powder, pepper, and salt.
4. Heat to boiling; reduce heat.
5. Stir in hot pasta.
6. Heat thoroughly.
7. Serve with Parmesan cheese, if desired.

Yields: 4 servings.

Calzone Pie

Our entire family loves calzone, and this easy-to-make calzone pie is very flavorful with the warm combination of adding wine, chocolate, and almonds to this meat pie.

Ingredients:

1 med. onion, chopped
2 lb. frozen bread dough, thawed
½ lb. ground beef
½ lb. ground pork
½ c. white wine
1 oz. semi-sweet chocolate, grated
⅓ c. almonds, chopped, toasted
3 egg whites, stiffly beaten
1 egg yolk, beaten
   salt and pepper, to taste

Directions:

1. Preheat oven to 400 degrees F.
2. In large, nonstick skillet, sauté onion.
3. Stir in meat; season to taste with salt and pepper.
4. Add wine; simmer until liquid is evaporated.
5. Stir in chocolate and almonds.
6. Over low heat, simmer 30 minutes, stirring occasionally.
7. Fold in egg whites; remove from heat.
8. Pat bread dough into two equal circles, using a rolling pin as needed.
9. Place one circle in a greased pie plate.
10. Pour meat mixture into pie plate; top with other dough circle, pressing to seal edges.
11. Prick top of dough using fork.
12. Brush top with egg yolk.
13. Bake 20 minutes.
14. Serve immediately.

Pork Chops Mole

My husband loves pork chops, and these pork chops with mole sauce and chocolate is a refreshing change of pace. Do try this recipe to serve for a special dinner for those who enjoy pork chops cooked a different way.

Ingredients:

4 pork chops (boned loin chops, ½-inch thick)
½ c. water
1 c. onion, chopped
½ c. yellow bell pepper, cut into strips
½ c. red bell pepper, cut into strips
1 Tbs. jalapeño pepper, seeded, minced
1 can tomatoes, diced, with garlic and onions,
  undrained, (14.5 oz.)
½ oz semi-sweet chocolate, grated
1 tsp. chili powder
1 tsp. dried oregano
½ tsp. salt
¼ tsp. cumin seed
½ c. fresh cilantro, minced
  canola cooking spray

Directions:

1. Lightly spray a large, nonstick skillet with cooking spray; heat over medium-high heat.
2. Cook chops 4 minutes on each side, or until browned; remove from pan.
3. Add water to pan, scraping to loosen browned bits.
4. Pour mixture over chops, cover, and set aside.
5. Reheat pan; add onion, bell pepper strips, and jalapeño. Cook 4 minutes, or until tender.
6. Stir in tomatoes; cook 1 more minute.
7. Add chocolate, chili powder, oregano, salt, and cumin.
8. Add chops and bring to boil; cover.
9. Reduce heat to medium-low; cook 5 minutes, stirring occasionally.
10. Sprinkle with cilantro.

Chicken with Mole Sauce

Cooking chicken pieces in a flavorful mole sauce is actually very delicious, and a nice change of pace.

Ingredients:

¼ c. flour
½ tsp. salt
½ tsp. black pepper, freshly ground
4 lb. chicken pieces
2 Tbs. olive oil
1 sm. onion, chopped
2 garlic cloves, minced
3 Tbs. fresh cilantro, chopped, divided
1¼ c. defatted chicken stock or water, divided
2 canned or fresh plum tomatoes, coarsely chopped
1 bay leaf
½ tsp. dried thyme
½ tsp. cinnamon
¼ c. pepitas (green pumpkin seeds)
½ mild chili pepper, dried
1 chipotle pepper, or to taste, seeds removed
½ oz. unsweetened chocolate, chopped

Directions:

1. In shallow baking dish, combine flour, salt, and pepper.
2. Dredge chicken pieces in flour mixture.
3. Heat oil in a deep casserole dish with a lid over medium-high heat.
4. Brown chicken in batches, turning, for about 5 minutes; set aside.
5. Add onions, garlic, 1 tablespoon cilantro, and ¼ cup stock or water to a pot.
6. Cook 2 minutes, or until softened.

7. Add tomatoes, bay leaf, thyme, cinnamon, and remaining stock or water.
8. Return chicken to the pot.
9. Bring to boil, reduce heat, and cover.
10. Simmer, basting occasionally, for 20 to 30 minutes, or until chicken is tender and juices run clear when pierced with a fork.
11. Meanwhile, roast pepitas over medium heat in a small, dry skillet, stirring frequently, for 3 minutes, or until lightly browned; set aside.
12. Roast pasilla and chipotle peppers in the same skillet for 30 to 40 seconds, or until fragrant.
13. Remove chicken from casserole dish; cool slightly.
14. Cover with tinfoil to keep warm; set aside.
15. Boil the sauce over high heat for 5 to 10 minutes, stirring often, until it has been reduced to 1 cup.
16. Add pepitas, dried peppers, and chipotles to the cooking liquid, and cook 1 to 2 minutes.
17. Remove bay leaf.
18. Transfer the sauce to a blender or food processor.
19. Add chocolate; blend until smooth.
20. If sauce seems too thick, add a little stock or water.
21. Return sauce to the casserole dish; heat through briefly over low heat.
22. Taste for seasoning: it should be smoky, hot, and slightly bitter.
23. Cover chicken with the sauce.
24. Garnish with the remaining cilantro.

Did You Know? . . . .

Did you know that you should not throw away your candy mold when you are done? Instead, make molded crayons! Take off the wrappers of the crayons, microwave in a paper bowl or cup for 4 to 5 minutes until melted, and pour into mold. You can use solid colors or swirl the colors together. Put in freezer for 15 to 20 minutes. Makes a great gift!

Grilled Turkey Mole

This is a wonderful way to serve turkey. The chocolate in this recipe adds a whole new flavor to the meat.

Ingredients:

- 6   turkey breast tenderloins, rinsed, dried
- ¼   c. lime juice
- 1   Tbs. chili powder
- 2   tsp. hot pepper sauce
- 1   Tbs. butter
- ½   c. onion, chopped
- 2   tsp. sugar
- 1   garlic clove
- 1   c. canned tomatoes, undrained, cut up
- ¼   c. green chili peppers, canned, diced
- 1½ tsp. unsweetened cocoa powder
- 1½ tsp. chili powder
- ⅛   tsp. salt
-     sour cream

Directions:

1. In small bowl, combine lime juice and hot pepper sauce; pour over turkey in resealable plastic bag.
2. Marinate in refrigerator for 2 to 4 hours, turning bag occasionally.
3. In medium saucepan, over high heat, sauté onion, sugar, and garlic in butter, 7 minutes, or until onion is tender.
4. Stir in tomatoes, chili peppers, cocoa powder, chili powder, and salt.
5. Bring to boil; reduce heat.
6. Cover; simmer 10 minutes.
7. Remove from heat; set aside.
8. Drain turkey, discard marinade.
9. Grill turkey on lightly greased grill, directly over medium heat for 8 to 10 minutes, or until turkey is tender and no longer pink, turning once.
10. Serve with sauce and sour cream.

Chili Con Cocoa

Cocoa and spices add great flavor to this meat chili, and makes a nice presentation served in hollowed out bread bowls.

Ingredients:

- ¼ c. canola oil
- 1½ c. onion, chopped
- 2 lb. ground beef or ground turkey
- 2 Tbs. cocoa
- 2 Tbs. chili powder
- 2 tsp. ground cayenne pepper
- 1 tsp. salt
- ½ tsp. ground allspice
- ½ tsp. ground cinnamon
- 7 c. whole tomatoes, undrained
- 1⅓ c. tomato paste
- 1 c. water
- ½ c. mini kisses milk chocolates
- 3 c. dark red kidney beans, undrained
- 14 mini bread bowls, hollowed out (8 oz. ea.)

Directions:

1. In large saucepan, heat oil over medium heat.
2. Add onion and cook, stirring frequently, 3 minutes or until tender.
3. Add meat, cook until brown; drain.
4. Stir in cocoa, chili powder, cayenne pepper, salt, allspice, cinnamon, tomatoes with liquid, tomato paste, and water; heat to boiling.
5. Reduce heat.
6. Add chocolate pieces and beans; simmer 30 minutes.
7. Ladle 1 cup chili into prepared bread bowls.
8. Garnish as desired.

Chili Gostoso

This chili is full of flavor with the addition of spices, peppers, mushrooms, and a hearty stew meat. It is a complete meal in itself, and great served with a side salad and your favorite bread or roll.

Ingredients:

2 lb. stew beef, cubed
2 lg. onions, chopped
3 celery, sliced
1 green bell pepper, chopped
1 red bell pepper, chopped
1 c. mushrooms, sliced
2 jalapeño peppers, chopped
4 garlic cloves, minced
3 Tbs. olive oil
2 Tbs. cocoa
2 Tbs. chili powder
1 tsp. ground cumin
1 tsp. dried oregano
1 tsp. paprika
1 tsp. ground turmeric
½ tsp. salt
½ tsp. ground cardamom
¼ tsp. pepper
1 Tbs. molasses
½ c. dry red wine
2 cans whole tomatoes, chopped, undrained (16 oz. ea.)
1 can kidney beans, drained (15 oz.)
1 can garbanzo beans, drained (15 oz.)
   sour cream, for garnish
   Cheddar cheese, shredded, for garnish

Directions:

1. In Dutch oven, heat oil.
2. Add beef, onions, celery, peppers, mushrooms, jalapeños, and garlic; stir until meat is browned.
3. Drain fat.

214

4. Stir in cocoa, cumin, oregano, paprika, turmeric, salt, cardamom, pepper, molasses, wine, tomatoes, and beans.
5. Bring mixture to boil; cover and reduce heat.
6. Simmer 1½ to 2 hours, stirring occasionally.
7. Serve with sour cream and cheese.

Chili Mole

This is another version of chili that is easy to make. This is made with unsweetened cocoa and simple spices to give it flavor.

Ingredients:

1   Tbs. canola oil
2   lb. ground beef
2   onions, chopped
2   garlic cloves, minced
2   cans kidney beans (15 oz. ea.)
2   cans tomato sauce (15 oz. ea.)
1¼ c. picanté sauce
½   c. water
3   Tbs. unsweetened cocoa
2   tsp. ground cumin
1   tsp. dried oregano, crushed
1¼ tsp. salt
⅛   tsp. ground cloves
⅛   tsp. nutmeg
⅛   tsp. allspice
1   green pepper, chopped

Directions:

1. In Dutch oven, heat oil; brown ground beef; drain.
2. Stir in onion and garlic.
3. Add beans, tomato sauce, picanté, water, cocoa, cumin, oregano, salt, cloves, nutmeg, and allspice; bring to boil.
4. Reduce heat; simmer 45 minutes.
5. Stir in green pepper.
6. Simmer 25 to 30 minutes more.

Chocolate Chili

This chili is unique in that it adds corn and bulgur with the addition of spices and cocoa to make a hearty chocolate chili.

Ingredients:

3 Tbs. canola oil
3 med. onions, chopped
1 Tbs. chili powder
1 Tbs. ground cumin
¼ tsp. cayenne pepper
2 med. green bell peppers, chopped
3 garlic cloves, finely chopped
3 Tbs. unsweetened cocoa powder
1 can tomatoes, diced, undrained (28 oz.)
1 c. water
1 can red kidney beans, drained, rinsed (14 oz.)
1 can black beans, drained, rinsed (14 oz.)
2 c. whole kernel corn, fresh or frozen
½ c. bulgur
    salt and pepper, to taste
    plain low fat yogurt
    fresh cilantro, chopped

Directions:

1. In large, heavy saucepan, heat oil over medium heat.
2. Add onions, chili powder, cumin, and cayenne pepper; sauté 5 minutes, or until onions are tender, stirring occasionally.
3. Add green peppers and garlic; sauté 1 minute.
4. Add cocoa, tomatoes, and water; stir well.
5. Bring to boil; add kidney beans, black beans, corn, and bulgur; mix well.
6. Reduce heat to low; simmer, uncovered, 15 minutes, or until bulgur is cooked.
7. Add salt and pepper, to taste.
8. To serve, top with a dollop of yogurt and sprinkle with cilantro.

Spicy Chicken Pumpkin Chili

Pumpkin adds an unusual flavor to this spicy chocolate chili. This makes an excellent autumn dish that will delight your family or guests.

Ingredients:

2 Tbs. olive oil
2 c. onion, chopped
2 c. red bell pepper, chopped
3 Tbs. jalapeño pepper, seeded, minced
1 garlic clove, crushed
1 c. beer
1 c. chicken broth
½ c. sliced ripe olives
3 Tbs. chili powder
1 tsp. ground coriander
½ tsp. salt
1 can tomatoes, chopped, undrained (29 oz.)
1 lb. boneless skinless chicken breasts, cut into pieces
2 c. fresh pumpkin, cooked
2 Tbs. fresh cilantro, chopped
1 Tbs. unsweetened cocoa
1 can pinto beans, drained (16 oz.)
6 Tbs. green onions, sliced
½ c. Cheddar cheese, sharp, shredded
6 Tbs. sour cream

Directions:

1. Heat oil in large Dutch oven over medium heat; add onion. Sauté 8 minutes, or until lightly browned.
2. Add bell pepper, jalapeño, and garlic; sauté 5 minutes.
3. Add beer, chicken broth, olives, chili powder, coriander, salt, tomatoes, and chicken pieces.
4. Bring to boil; partially cover and reduce heat.
5. Simmer 20 minutes, or until chicken is done.
6. Stir in pumpkin, cilantro, cocoa, and beans.
7. Cook 5 minutes.
8. Top with green onions, cheese, and sour cream.

Turkey Chili

Try this savory chili. This makes a spicy chili as a change of pace from plain chili.

Ingredients:

    6 Tbs. olive oil, divided
    1 lg. yellow onion, chopped
    6 garlic cloves, minced
    2 Tbs. cumin seed
    2 red bell pepper, chopped
    2 poblano peppers, chopped
    2 jalapeños, seeded, chopped
    2 serrano chilies, seeded, chopped
    1 c. ancho chili paste
    3 Tbs. chili powder
    1 Tbs. ground coriander
    1 Tbs. cinnamon
    1 Tbs. black pepper
    2 lb. ground turkey
    4 c. tomatoes with juice, chopped
    2 c. chicken stock
    1 c. beer
    7 oz. chipotle peppers in adobo sauce
    ¼ c. unsweetened chocolate, grated
      chopped green onion, cilantro, grated cheese,
      fried tortilla strips, and sour cream, for garnish

Directions:

1. In Dutch oven, heat 3 tablespoons of oil; sauté onion, garlic, and cumin seeds until onions are soft.
2. Stir in peppers; sauté 10 minutes.
3. Add chili paste, chili powder, coriander, cinnamon, and pepper; sauté 5 to 7 minutes, stirring frequently.
4. In large skillet, heat remaining oil; brown ground turkey and drain fat.
5. Combine pepper mixture, turkey, tomatoes, chicken stock, beer, and chipotle peppers in Dutch oven; simmer 45 to 60 minutes. Stir in chocolate.
6. Garnish with green onions, cilantro, cheese, tortilla strips, and sour cream.

Chocolate Delights

A Collection of Chocolate Recipes
Cookbook Delights Series Book 3

Pies

Table of Contents

A Basic Recipe for Pie Crust

This is a very good recipe for a delicious, flaky crust.

Ingredients for single crust:

> 1½ c. sifted all-purpose flour
> ½   tsp. salt
> ½   c. shortening
> 4-5 Tbs. ice water

Ingredients for double crust:

> 2   c. sifted all-purpose flour
> 1   tsp. salt
> ⅔   c. shortening
> 5-7 Tbs. ice water

Directions for single crust:

1. In large bowl stir together flour and salt.
2. Cut in shortening with pastry blender or mix with fingertips until pieces are size of coarse crumbs.
3. Sprinkle 2 tablespoons ice water over flour mixture, tossing with fork.
4. Add just enough remaining water 1 tablespoon at a time to moisten dough, tossing so dough holds together.
5. Roll pastry into 11-inch circle, and wrap in plastic wrap; refrigerate for 1 hour.
6. Preheat oven to 425 degrees F.
7. Remove plastic wrap from pastry, and fit pastry into a 9-inch pie plate.
8. Fold edge under and then crimp between thumb and forefinger to make fluted crust.
9. For filled pie with an instant or cooked filling (cream-filled, custard-filled, etc.), prick crust all over with fork then bake 15 to 20 minutes until done.
10. If preparing pie with uncooked filling (such as pumpkin), do not prick crust; pour filling into unbaked pastry shell, and then bake as directed.

Directions for double crust:

1. Turn desired filling into pastry-lined pie plate; trim overhanging edge of pastry ½ inch from rim of plate.
2. Cut slits with knife in top crust for steam vents.
3. Place over filling; trim overhanging edge of pastry 1 inch from rim of plate.
4. Fold and roll top edge under lower edge, pressing on rim to seal; flute.
5. Cover fluted edge with 2- to 3-inch-wide strip of aluminum foil to prevent excessive browning.
6. Remove foil during last 15 minutes of baking.

Yields: 1 pie crust (9-inch single or double).

A Basic Cookie or Graham Cracker Crust

This is a great crust for use with cream pies or for an unbaked pie. Use your favorite flavor of cookie to complement your filling, or use graham crackers.

Ingredients:

2 c. cookie or graham cracker crumbs, finely crushed
⅓ c. sugar
½ c. butter, melted

Directions:

1. Combine crumbs, sugar, and butter.
2. Press mixture firmly against bottom and up sides of 9-inch pie plate.
3. Baking is not necessary, but if preferred crust may be baked at 400 degrees F. for 10 minutes.

Yields: 1 pie crust (9-inch).

Black Bottom Pie

This is a rich, elegant-looking chocolate pie and a welcome treat for any occasion.

Ingredients:

1 chocolate cookie crumb crust (9-inch) (see page 221)
½ c. sugar
⅓ c. unsweetened cocoa
¼ c. butter
1 pkg. unflavored gelatin
¼ c. cold water
½ c. sugar
¼ c. cornstarch
2 c. milk
5 eggs, separated
1 tsp. vanilla extract
1 tsp. rum
½ c. sugar
   chocolate, grated

Directions:

1. In medium bowl, combine sugar, cocoa, and butter.
2. In small bowl, combine gelatin and cold water.
3. Place bowl in pan of simmering water to dissolve gelatin.
4. In medium saucepan, combine sugar, cornstarch, milk, and egg yolks.
5. Cook over medium heat, stirring constantly until mixture boils; boil and stir 1 minute.
6. Remove from heat; measure 1½ cup of the mixture, and blend into cocoa-sugar mixture.
7. Add vanilla; pour into cooled crust; chill until set.
8. Combine dissolved gelatin with remaining custard; stir in rum.
9. In medium bowl, beat egg whites until foamy.
10. Gradually add sugar; beat until stiff peaks form.

11. Fold gelatin-custard mixture into beaten egg whites.
12. Chill 15 minutes, or until partially set.
13. Spoon over chocolate custard in prepared crust.
14. Chill until set.
15. Garnish with grated chocolate before serving.

Irish Cream Chocolate Pie

This pie is a popular holiday favorite and very delicious. Your guests will enjoy this delightful treat.

Ingredients:

1 graham or chocolate crust (see page 221)
1 pkg. unflavored gelatin
1 tsp. vanilla extract
¾ c. milk
¾ c. Irish Cream
1 pkg. semi-sweet chocolate chips (6 oz.)
2 c. whipped cream, sweetened
    chocolate-dipped strawberries, for garnish

Directions:

1. In small saucepan, sprinkle gelatin over milk; let stand 1 minute.
2. Stir over low heat until gelatin is dissolved, about 5 minutes.
3. Add chocolate and continue cooking, stirring constantly until chocolate is melted; stir in vanilla.
4. Remove from heat; stir occasionally, adding Irish Cream about 5 minutes after removal from heat.
5. When mixture forms mounds when dropped from spoon, fold in sweetened whipped cream.
6. Turn into crust.
7. Garnish with more whipped cream and strawberries if desired.
8. Chill 4 hours before serving.

Double Chocolate Fruit Tart

I love fruit tarts with fresh fruit and preserves, and this particular recipe uses apricot preserves as a base to contrast nicely with chocolate. It is very good, and do enjoy.

Ingredients for chocolate crumb crust:

1½ c. vanilla wafer crumbs
⅓ c. cocoa
⅓ c. powdered sugar
½ c. butter, melted

Ingredients for tart:

1 pkg. cream cheese, softened (8 oz.)
½ c. sugar
3 Tbs. cocoa
1 Tbs. milk
1½ tsp. vanilla extract
¼ c. peach or apricot preserves
assorted fresh fruit (strawberries, kiwifruit etc.)

Directions for chocolate crumb crust:

1. Butter bottom and side of 12-inch pizza pan.
2. In medium bowl, combine crumbs, cocoa, and powdered sugar.
3. Stir in butter.
4. Press mixture onto bottom and up side of prepared pan.
5. Chill thoroughly.

Directions for tart:

1. In medium bowl, beat cream cheese, sugar, cocoa, milk, and vanilla until smooth and well blended.
2. Spread mixture over prepared crust.

3. Refrigerate until chilled.
4. Arrange fruit on cream cheese mixture.
5. Heat preserves until thin; cool slightly.
6. Glaze fruit with preserves.
7. Refrigerate until set.
8. Cut into wedges.

Creamy Chocolate Tarts

Here is another version of tarts using whipped cream and fresh fruit.

Ingredients:

⅔ c. semi-sweet chocolate chips
¼ c. milk
1 Tbs. sugar
½ tsp. vanilla extract
½ c. whipping cream, cold
6 single-serve graham cracker crusts (see page 221)
   sweetened whipped cream
   fresh fruit, cherries or mint, for garnish

Directions:

1. In small microwaveable bowl, place chocolate chips, milk, and sugar.
2. Microwave on high 1 minute until milk is hot and chips melt when stirred.
3. With wire whisk or rotary beater, beat until mixture is smooth; stir in vanilla.
4. Cool to room temperature.
5. In small bowl, beat whipping cream until stiff.
6. Carefully fold chocolate mixture into whipped cream until blended.
7. Spoon or pipe into crusts, cover.
8. Refrigerate until set.
9. Top with sweetened whipped cream.
10. Garnish as desired.

Chocolate Pie

My mom always used to make this for my dad, and, of course, we all enjoyed it. This is a great treat for chocolate lovers.

Ingredients:

> 2 c. sugar
> 5 Tbs. unsweetened cocoa powder
> ¼ c. flour
> 1 can evaporated milk
> 1 tsp. vanilla extract
> 4 lg. eggs, separated
> ¼ c. butter
> ¼ c. sugar
> 1 9-inch single crust pie (see page 220)

Directions:

1. Preheat oven to 350 degrees F.
2. In medium saucepan, whisk together sugar, cocoa and flour.
3. Blend in milk and vanilla.
4. In small bowl, beat egg yolks.
5. Stir into sugar mixture.
6. Over low heat, heat, stirring constantly, just until butter is melted.
7. Pour filling into unbaked pie shell.
8. Bake 35 to 40 minutes, or until pie is not wobbly when shaken.
9. In small bowl, beat egg whites until soft peaks form.
10. Gradually add ¼ cup sugar, beating constantly, until stiff peaks form.
11. Spread meringue on pie.
12. Return pie to oven.
13. Bake until meringue is golden.
14. Cut into wedges.

Strawberry Chocolate Tart

Strawberries and chocolate are always a welcome combination in our family. This is an elegant way to serve a company dessert or special event for the family. Serve with sweetened whipped cream for a delicious delight.

Ingredients:

¾ c. butter, softened
½ c. powdered sugar
1½ c. flour
½ c. milk
2 egg yolks, beaten
¼ c. sugar
¼ tsp. salt
2 c. semi-sweet or milk chocolate chips
1 pt. fresh strawberries, rinsed, hulled (2 c.)

Directions:

1. Preheat oven to 350 degrees F.
2. In small bowl, beat butter and powdered sugar until smooth; blend in flour.
3. Press mixture onto bottom and up sides of 9½-inch or 11-inch round tart pan with removable bottom.
4. Bake 20 to 25 minutes, or until lightly browned.
5. Cool completely.
6. In medium microwaveable bowl, microwave milk on high 1 to 1½ minutes, until hot, but not boiling.
7. With wire whisk, stir in egg yolks, sugar and salt.
8. Microwave on high 30 seconds at a time, stirring after each heating, until hot, smooth, and slightly thickened.
9. Stir in chocolate chips until melted and mixture is smooth; pour into prepared crust.
10. Place plastic wrap directly onto surface; refrigerate until firm.
11. Remove plastic wrap from filling; cut strawberries into ¼-inch slices; arrange over top of tart.
12. Serve cold.
13. Refrigerate leftover tart.

Chocolate Coconut Lime Pie

The flavors in this pie blend to make a delicious dessert for family or friends.

Ingredients:

- 1 Tbs. unflavored gelatin
- 1 cup sugar, divided
- ¼ tsp. salt
- 5 eggs, separated
- ½ c. lime juice, strained
- ¼ c. water
- 1 tsp. lime peel, grated
- ½ c. coconut, shredded
- 1 c. heavy cream, whipped
- 1 9-inch chocolate graham cracker crust (see page 221) grated chocolate and lime slices, for garnish

Directions:

1. In small saucepan, mix gelatin, ½ cup of sugar, and salt.
2. In small bowl, beat egg yolks.
3. Add lime juice and water to egg yolks.
4. Stir egg yolk mixture into gelatin mixture.
5. Cook on low heat, stirring, just until mixture comes to a boil.
6. Remove from heat; blend in grated peel, and coconut.
7. Chill, blending often, until mixture is thick when dropped by spoon.
8. In small bowl, beat egg whites until soft peaks form.
9. Add remaining sugar and beat until stiff.
10. Fold into gelatin mixture.
11. Fold in whipped cream.
12. Pour into crust; refrigerate until firm.
13. Serve with a sprinkle of chocolate and garnish with lime slice.

Chocolate Banana Cream Pie

My mom and dad always enjoyed chocolate cream pie. My mom would make it for family and guests quite often, and now my own son Kyler and my daughter Kelsey often request this pie with the addition of bananas.

Ingredients:

4 lg. egg yolks
1½ c. sugar
⅓ c. cornstarch
½ tsp. salt
3 c. milk
2 oz. unsweetened baking chocolate
2 Tbs. butter, softened
1 Tbs. plus 1 tsp. vanilla extract
2 lg. bananas
1 9-inch pie crust, baked (see page 220)
toffee bits, for garnish

Directions:

1. In medium bowl, beat egg yolks with fork; set aside.
2. In 2-quart saucepan, mix sugar, cornstarch, and salt; gradually stir in milk.
3. Cook over medium heat, stirring constantly, until mixture thickens and comes to a boil; boil 1 minute.
4. Immediately stir at least half of the hot mixture gradually into egg yolks, and then stir yolk mixture back into remaining hot mixture in the saucepan.
5. Boil and stir 1 minute; remove from heat and cool to lukewarm.
6. Slice 2 large bananas into pie crust; pour warm filling over bananas.
7. Refrigerate 2 hours until set; cut into wedges.
8. Garnish each serving with a dollop of whipped cream, toffee bits, and banana slices if desired.

Chocolate Raspberry Cheesecake Pie

This chocolate raspberry cheesecake pie is wonderful.

Ingredients for chocolate crust:

  1½ c. chocolate cookie crumbs
  1   Tbs. sugar
  ¼ c. butter, melted

Ingredients for chocolate glaze:

  2   sq. semi-sweet baking chocolate (1 oz. ea.)
  ¼ c. whipping cream

Ingredients for cheesecake filling:

  1   chocolate pie crust (recipe above)
  2   pkg. cream cheese, softened (3 oz. ea.)
  1   can sweetened condensed milk (14 oz.)
  1   egg
  1   tsp. vanilla extract
  1   can raspberries, drained

Directions for chocolate crust:

1. In medium bowl, combine ingredients until thoroughly blended.
2. Press into 9-inch pie pan.

Direction for chocolate glaze:

1. In small saucepan, combine cream and chocolate.
2. Cook over low heat stirring constantly until chocolate melts and mixture thickens slightly.
3. Remove from heat, pour over cooled cheesecake, and cool for 30 minutes.
4. Refrigerate at least 2 hours.
5. Garnish with a few raspberries.
6. Store in refrigerator.

Directions for cheesecake filling:

1. Preheat oven to 350 degrees F.
2. In medium bowl, with electric mixer, beat cream cheese until fluffy.
3. Gradually beat in milk until smooth.
4. Add egg and vanilla; mix well.
5. Arrange raspberries in bottom of chocolate crust.
6. Slowly pour cream cheese mixture over berries.
7. Bake 30 to 35 minutes, or until center is almost set.
8. Cool 1 hour.

Chocolate Peaches and Cream Pie

Here is a delightful and delicious pie that your family will really enjoy on a hot summer day. Our family loves the flavors blended together in this one.

Ingredients:

½ c. chocolate syrup
1 graham cracker crust (see page 221)
1 qt. peach or vanilla ice cream, softened
1 fresh peach, peeled, sliced
¼ c. pecan halves, toasted
   additional chocolate syrup

Directions:

1. Prepare graham cracker crust.
2. Spread chocolate syrup over pie crust.
3. Spoon ice cream on top of syrup; spread evenly.
4. Cover; place in freezer for 3 hours, or until firm.
5. Let stand 15 minutes at room temperature before cutting into wedges.
6. Place each wedge onto individual serving dishes.
7. Top with peach slices and pecan halves; drizzle with additional chocolate syrup.

Yields: 8 servings.

Frozen Grasshopper Pie

Step three is an important step that I sometimes try to rush, and it does not work. The marshmallow mixture must be totally cooled, or it will wilt the whipped cream and will not be as tasty as it should be. This pie is always great to have stashed away in the freezer for unexpected company or an unplanned dessert.

Ingredients:

    16 chocolate sandwich cookies, crushed
    2   Tbs. butter, melted
    ⅓   c. sugar
    2⅔ c. hot milk
    1⅓ c. crème de menthe
    ¾   c. crème de cacao
    2   c. miniature marshmallows
    6   c. whipped cream, beaten

Directions:

1. In medium bowl, combine sandwich cookies and sugar with butter.
2. Press mixture into pie pan to form chocolate crust.
3. Melt marshmallows in hot milk; cool to lukewarm.
4. Add crème de menthe and cacao; blend well.
5. Place mixture into refrigerator until chilled; blend in whipping cream.
6. Pour filling into chocolate crust.
7. Chill until ready to serve.

Did You Know? . . . .

Did you know for faster cooling of chocolate and for that fine, professional, finished look, put your mold, filled with warm chocolate, in the freezer, and dipped items in the refrigerator. Be sure to do this before they start to harden up, or the chocolate will look a bit foggy instead of shiny.

Midnight Madness Pie

This is another rich chocolate pie that is easy to make and tastes great.

Ingredients for chocolate crust:

    1½ c. chocolate wafer crumbs
    ¼ c. butter, melted

Ingredients for filling:

    1   pkg. cream cheese, softened (8 oz.)
    ½   c. mayonnaise
    ½   c. sugar
    2   eggs
    1   pkg. semi-sweet chocolate chips, melted
    1   tsp. vanilla extract

Directions for chocolate crust:

1. Preheat oven to 350 degrees F.
2. In small bowl, combine crumbs and butter; reserve 3 tablespoons for topping if desired.
3. Press remaining mixture firmly against bottom and side of pie plate.
4. Chill until firm in refrigerator or bake for 10 minutes; cool.

Directions for filling:

1. Preheat oven to 350 degrees F.
2. In large bowl, with mixer on medium speed, beat cream cheese and mayonnaise until smooth.
3. Gradually beat in sugar; beat in eggs one at a time.
4. Add chocolate and vanilla; beat until smooth.
5. Pour into prepared pie crust; place on baking sheet.
6. Bake 30 to 35 minutes, or until set.
7. Chill 4 hours before serving.

Chocolate Coconut Macaroon Tarts

The flavors of these little cups of toasted coconut are delicious and easy to make. Enjoy!

Ingredients:

- ¾ c. sugar
- ½ c. egg whites (from 3 eggs)
- 2½ c. coconut, sweetened, flaked or desiccated
- ½ c. heavy cream
- 8   oz. semi-sweet chocolate, chopped
- 24 mini muffin cups or individual tart molds
    few toasted almonds, chopped, for garnish

Directions for filling:

1. In small bowl, place chopped chocolate.
2. In small saucepan, heat cream until just boiling.
3. Pour over chocolate; let sit for 1 minute.
4. Whisk gently until glossy to melt chocolate completely.

Directions for tarts:

1. Preheat oven to 350 degrees F.
2. In medium bowl, mix sugar, egg whites, and coconut together.
3. Put a spoonful in each cup or mold.
4. Press into the molds to make little cups, with sides and a well for holding the chocolate filling.
5. Bake 30 minutes, until golden.
6. Cool completely in pans; remove gently.
7. Make the filling and pour over tarts.
8. Sprinkle a few pieces of chopped almonds in the center of each tart while warm.
9. Let set at room temperature, 1 hour before serving.
10. Note: Chocolate can be refrigerated up to 5 days.
11. Tart shells can be baked up to 2 days in advance.

12. Store at room temperature in an airtight container.
13. Rewarm in microwave or bowl set over simmering water and pour over tarts.

Chocolate Cheese Pie

This truly decadent cheesecake-type dessert is sure to please all chocoholics everywhere!

Ingredients:

  1 pkg. cream cheese (8 oz.), softened
  1 pkg. cream cheese (3 oz.), softened
  ¾ c. sugar
  ½ c. baking cocoa
  2 eggs
  1 tsp. vanilla extract
  ½ c. whipping cream, cold
  1 unbaked chocolate crumb crust (see page 221)
    cherry pie filling or sliced fresh fruit

Directions:

  1. Preheat oven to 350 degrees F.
  2. Beat cream cheese and sugar in large bowl until well blended.
  3. Add cocoa; beat until well blended, scraping sides of bowl and beaters frequently.
  4. Add eggs and beat well.
  5. Stir in vanilla and whipping cream.
  6. Pour into prepared crust.
  7. Bake 35 to 40 minutes (center will be soft but will set upon cooling).
  8. Cool to room temperature.
  9. Cover; refrigerate several hours or overnight.
  10. When ready to serve, spoon pie filling or fresh fruit over pie.
  11. Cover and refrigerate any leftover pie.

Chocolate Chiffon Pie

Chocolate chiffon pie is an elegant dish to add to your any meal.

Ingredients:

- 1 pkg. unflavored gelatin
- ¼ c. water, cold
- ½ c. water, boiling
- 6 Tbs. baking cocoa
- 4 eggs, separated
- 1 c. sugar, divided
- ¼ tsp. salt
- 1 tsp. vanilla extract
- 1 single-crust pie shell (9-inch), baked (see page 220)

Directions:

1. Prepare pie shell.
2. Pour cold water in small bowl and sprinkle gelatin on top.
3. In large bowl, mix boiling water and cocoa until smooth.
4. Add softened gelatin to hot cocoa mixture; stir until dissolved.
5. Add egg yolks, slightly beaten, ½ cup sugar, salt, and vanilla; cool.
6. While mixture is cooling, beat egg whites until soft peaks form.
7. Gradually add remaining sugar and beat until stiff peaks form.
8. When chocolate mixture begins to thicken, fold in beaten egg whites.
9. Fill baked pie shell and chill.

Yields: 6 to 8 servings.

Chocolate Mud Pie

This pie is easy to make, tastes good, and will disappear quickly.

Ingredients for crust:

8   whole honey graham crackers, finely crushed (about 1¼ c. crumbs)

¼   c. sugar

⅓   c. butter

Ingredients for filling:

1   jar chocolate fudge sauce (12 oz.)

1½ pt. orange sherbet

½   c. miniature chocolate chips

Directions for crust:

1. Preheat oven to 375 degrees F.
2. Mix all ingredients until well blended.
3. Press firmly onto bottom and up side of 9-inch pie plate.
4. Bake 8 to 10 minutes or until lightly browned.
5. Cool completely.

Directions for filling:

1. Using rubber spatula, spread chocolate fudge sauce evenly over cooled pie crust.
2. Place in freezer to harden.
3. Remove sherbet from freezer to soften.
4. In medium bowl, combine sherbet and chocolate chips.
5. Spoon sherbet mixture into prepared crust.
6. Smooth top with spatula.
7. Return to freezer until ready to serve.

Chocolate Stout Silk Pie

This is a very rich, creamy pie. The stout is a wonderful complement to the chocolate.

Ingredients for crust:

    1½ c. crushed graham crackers
    ⅓ c. butter, melted

Ingredients for filling:

    12 oz. semi-sweet or bittersweet chocolate
    24 lg. marshmallows
    1   pinch salt
    ⅔ c. stout
    ⅓ c. evaporated milk
    1   tsp. vanilla extract
    1   Tbs. crème de cacao (light or dark)
        sweetened whipped cream

Directions for crust:

1. Preheat oven to 350 degrees F.
2. Add butter to graham cracker crumbs, and mix until well blended.
3. Press crust mixture into bottom and up sides of pie plate; bake about 6 minutes, until set.

Directions for filling:

1. Place chocolate, marshmallows, and salt in blender; blend until well mixed and chocolate is finely ground.
2. In 2 separate saucepans (in order to prevent curdling), heat stout and evaporated milk until very hot but not boiling.
3. Pour stout and milk into blender, and blend 1 minute.
4. Add vanilla and crème de cacao, and blend.
5. Pour into crust and refrigerate overnight.
6. Garnish with whipped cream.

Chocolate Delights
A Collection of Chocolate Recipes
Cookbook Delights Series Book 3

Preserving

Table of Contents

A Basic Guide for Canning, Dehydrating, and Freezing

1. Place empty jars in hot, soapy water. Wash well inside and out with brush or soft cloth.
2. Run your finger around rim of each jar, discarding any that are chipped or cracked.
3. Rinse in clean, clear, very hot water, being careful to use tongs to avoid burning skin or fingers.
4. Place upside down on towel or fabric to drain well.
5. Place lids in boiling water bath for 2 minutes to sterilize and keep hot until ready to place on jar rims.
6. Immediately prior to filling jars with hot food, immerse in hot bath for 1 minute to heat jars. Heating jars avoids breakage.
7. If filling with room-temperature food, you need not immerse immediately prior to filling.
8. Fill jars with food to within ½ inch of neck of jars.
9. When ladling liquid over food, fill jars to 1 inch from top rim in each jar. This leaves air allowance for sealing purposes.
10. Wipe rims of jars with damp, clean cloth to remove any particles of food and again check for chips or cracks.
11. Using tongs, place lids from hot bath directly onto jars.
12. Place rings over lids, and using cloth, gloves, or holders, tighten down firmly while hanging onto jars.
13. Do not tighten down too hard as air may become trapped in jars and prevent them from sealing.
14. For fruits, tomatoes, and pickled vegetables, place each jar into water bath canning kettle so water covers jars by at least 1 inch.
15. For vegetables, process them in a pressure canner according to manufacturer's directions.
16. Follow time recommended for food being canned.
17. Do not mix jars of food in same canning kettle as times may vary for each kind of food.

18. At end of time recommended for canning, gently lift each jar out of bath with tongs, and place on protected surface.
19. Turn lids gently to be sure they are firmly tight.
20. Place filled, ringed jars on cloth to cool gradually.
21. Do not disturb rings, lids, or jars until sealed.
22. Lids will show slight indentation when sealed.
23. When cool, wipe jars with damp cloth then label and date each jar.
24. Leave overnight until thoroughly cooled.
25. Jars may then be stored upright on shelves.

Dehydrating

1. Always begin with fresh, good quality food that is clean and inspected for damage.
2. Pretreatment is not necessary, but food that is blanched will keep its color and flavor better. Use the same blanching times as you would for freezing. Fruit, especially, responds to pretreatment.
3. Doing some research on pretreatments may help you decide what procedure you would like to use.
4. You can marinate, salt, sweeten, or spice foods before you dehydrate them.
5. Jerky is meat that has been marinated and/or flavored by rubbing spices into it; avoid oil or grease of any kind as it will turn rancid as the food dries.
6. Vegetables and fruit can be treated the same way.
7. Slice or dice food thin and uniform so that it will dehydrate evenly. Uneven thicknesses may cause food to spoil because it did not dry as thoroughly as other parts.
8. Space food on dehydrator tray so that air can move around each piece.
9. Try not to let any piece touch another.
10. Fill your trays with all the same type of food as different foods take different amounts of time to dry.

11. You can, of course, dry different types of food at the same time, but you will have to remember to watch and remove the food that dehydrates more quickly. You can mix different foods in the same dehydrator batch, but do not mix strong vegetables like onions and garlic as other foods will absorb their taste while they are dehydrating.

12. The smaller the pieces, the faster a food will dehydrate. Thin leaves of spinach, celery, etc., will dry fastest. Remove them from the stalks before drying them or they will be overdone, losing flavor and quality. In very warm areas, they might even scorch. If they do, they will taste just like burned food when you rehydrate them.

13. Dense food like carrots will feel very hard when they are ready. Others will be crispy. Usually, a food that is high in fructose (sugar) will be leathery when it is finished dehydrating.

14. Remember that food smells when it is in the process of drying, so outdoors or in the garage is an excellent place to dry a big batch of those onions!

15. Always test each batch to make sure it is "done."

16. You can pasteurize finished food by putting it in a slow oven (150 degrees F.) for a few minutes.

17. Let the food cool before storing.

18. Store in airtight containers to guard against moisture. Jars saved from other food work well as long as they have lids that will keep moisture out.

19. Zip-closure food storage bags work well.

20. Jars of dehydrated carrots, celery, beets, etc., may look cheerful on your countertop, but the colors and flavors will fade. Dehydrated food keeps its color and flavor best if stored in a dark, cool place.

21. Dehydrating food takes time, so do not rush it. When you are all done, you will have a dried food stash to be proud of.

Freezing

1. Wash all containers and lids in hot, soapy water using soft cloth.
2. Rinse well in clear, clean, hot water.
3. Cool and drain well.
4. Place food into container to within 1 inch of rim. This allows for expansion of food during freezing.
5. Wipe rim of container with clean damp cloth, checking for chips or breaks.
6. Be certain cover fits the container snugly to avoid leaks. Burp air from container.
7. If food is hot when placing in container, cool prior to placing in freezer.
8. Label and date each container.
9. Store upright in freezer until frozen solid.

Did You Know? . . . .

Did you know that cacao has been cultivated for three millennia in Central America and Mexico? Its earliest documented use is around 1100 BC.

Did you know all of the Mesoamerican peoples made chocolate beverages, including the Maya and Aztecs? They made it into a beverage known as xocolātl, a Nahuatl word meaning "bitter water". The seeds of the cacao tree have an intense bitter taste, and must be fermented to develop the flavor. After being roasted and ground, the resulting products are known as chocolate or cocoa.

Did you know there are 5 to 6 million cocoa farmers worldwide?

Chocolate Applesauce Bread

*The applesauce adds moisture to this chocolate bread,
and it also freezes well.*

Ingredients:

- 1 c. butter, room temperature
- 3 c. sugar
- 4 egg whites, beaten until foamy
- 1 Tbs. vanilla extract
- ½ tsp. almond extract
- 2 c. applesauce, room temperature
- 3 c. flour
- ¾ c. unsweetened cocoa, sift before measuring
- 1 tsp. baking soda
- ½ tsp. baking powder
- ⅛ tsp. salt

Directions:

1. Preheat oven to 325 degrees F.
2. Place baking sheet onto middle rack of oven and remove top rack from oven.
3. Prepare 8 (1-pint) wide mouth canning jars with lids as per manufacturer's instructions; cool jars. Keep lids in hot water until ready to use.
4. Generously grease jars with butter.
5. In mixing bowl, combine butter, sugar, egg whites, vanilla, almond extract, and applesauce.
6. In another mixing bowl, combine flour, cocoa, baking powder, baking soda, and salt.
7. Mix butter and egg mixture with dry ingredients just until moistened.
8. Spoon 1 cup of batter into each jar.
9. Carefully wipe rims clean.
10. Place jars on baking sheet in the center of oven.
11. Bake 40 minutes.
12. Remove jars from oven, one at a time.
13. Carefully put lids and rings in place, then screw tops on tightly.

14. Place jars on wire rack; they will seal as they cool.
15. These cakes are not really "canned", so be sure to make them just before giving.
16. Decorate jars as desired.
17. Give as gifts with instructions to serve immediately or freeze.

Freezer Chocolate Fudge Sauce

Try this chocolate fudge sauce which can be made and frozen. Many recipes say they are safe to be canned using a boiling water canner, but in studies by the University of Georgia on chocolate sauce, they caution canning chocolate because of its low acidity. If the pH is too low it becomes unsafe for canning, and to be safe for your family you might want to try freezing it.

Ingredients:

½   c. butter
2½ c. sugar
3   sq. unsweetened chocolate (3 oz.)
1   can evaporated milk (12 oz.)
1   tsp. vanilla extract
     salt, to taste

Directions:

1. In top of double boiler, melt butter.
2. Add chocolate and melt, while constantly stirring.
3. Add sugar gradually, ¼ cup at a time, while stirring.
4. Add salt.
5. Stir milk in gradually, then vanilla.
6. Cook 1 hour, or until desired thickness, stirring occasionally.
7. Pour sauce into clean, warm, wide mouth quart jar(s) or similar freezer-safe container(s).
8. Cool at room temperature 1 to 2 hours.
9. Seal and freeze.
10. Note: The sauce should remain soft enough to spoon out portions while frozen.

Chocolate Sauce

This is a delicious chocolate sauce that you can enjoy with variations of orange, mint, coffee, or raspberry flavor. Do try all the different varieties, and decide which is your favorite. Studies performed by the University of Georgia on chocolate sauce, say that caution should be taken canning chocolate because of its low acidity. If the pH is too low it becomes unsafe for canning, and to be safe for your family you might want to try freezing it.

Ingredients:

- 2 oz. semi-sweet baking chocolate
- 2 Tbs. butter
- ½ c. water, boiling
- 1½ c. sugar
- ⅛ tsp. salt
- 1 tsp. vanilla extract

Directions:

1. Preheat oven to 350 degrees F.
2. Melt chocolate in a glass or enamel double boiler.
3. Stir in butter, water, sugar, and salt.
4. Cook 15 minutes, stirring occasionally.
5. Remove from heat.
6. Stir in vanilla extract.
7. Serve warm; reheat 1 minute on high in microwave.
8. To store, pour into sterilized glass jars.
9. Allow sauce to cool before refrigerating.
10. Will keep for 6 months.
11. Variations: Add any of the following in place of, or in addition to, the vanilla extract: 1 teaspoon mint extract, 1 teaspoon orange extract or ⅓ cup orange juice, 1 teaspoon instant coffee, ⅛ cup crushed raspberries, 1 tablespoon crème de menthe or coffee liqueur, chopped strawberries, raisins, or nuts.

Hot Fudge Sauce

Remember when you can hot fudge sauce that the pH has to be safe for canning. Studies performed by the University of Georgia on chocolate sauce, say that caution should be taken canning chocolate because of its low acidity. If the pH is too low it becomes unsafe for canning, and to be safe for your family you might want to try freezing it. This particular hot fudge sauce is safe, and it can be tested with your own pH paper to make sure it is safe for canning.

Ingredients:

1 pkg. semi-sweet chocolate chips (6 oz.) **OR**
4 sq. semi-sweet chocolate, chunked (1 oz. ea.) **OR**
6 oz. fine quality bittersweet chocolate, chunked
2 Tbs. butter
1 can sweetened condensed milk (14 oz.)
2 Tbs. water
1 tsp. pure vanilla extract

Directions:

1. In heavy saucepan, place all ingredients; mix well.
2. Over medium heat, cook 5 minutes, and stir constantly until all is melted, well blended, and slightly thickened.
3. Pour into hot, sterilized jars; apply two-piece lids prepared according to manufacturer's instructions.
4. Process in boiling water bath for 15 minutes.
5. Remove jars; place on a folded towel or pad of newspaper in a draft free location; cool completely.
6. Remove rings, check seals, wash in warm soapy water, dry, label, and store in a cool, dry location.
7. Serve warm over ice cream and refrigerate leftovers.

Chocolate Raspberry Topping

Chocolate and raspberries make a great flavorful combination, and this topping is great served over homemade ice cream. Studies performed by the University of Georgia on chocolate sauce, say that caution should be taken canning chocolate because of its low acidity. If the pH is too low it becomes unsafe for canning, and to be safe for your family you might want to try freezing it.

Ingredients:

- ½   c. unsweetened cocoa powder, sifted
- 1   pkg. fruit pectin
- 4½ c. red raspberries, crushed
- 6¾ c. sugar
- 4   Tbs. lemon juice

Directions:

1. Prepare boiling water canner.
2. Prepare jars and lids as per manufacturer's instructions. Set bands aside.
3. In medium glass bowl, combine cocoa powder and pectin, stirring until evenly blended; set aside.
4. In large stainless steel saucepan, combine raspberries and lemon juice.
5. Whisk in pectin mixture until dissolved.
6. Over high heat, bring to boil stirring frequently.
7. Add sugar all at once; return to full rolling boil, stirring constantly.
8. Boil hard for 1 minute, stirring constantly.
9. Remove from heat and skim off foam.
10. Ladle into hot jars leaving ¼-inch headspace.
11. Remove air bubbles; wipe rim and center lid on jar.
12. Apply band until fit is fingertip tight.
13. Process in boiling water canner for 10 minutes, adjusting for altitude; remove jars and cool.

Yields: 6 (8 oz.) half-pints.

Chocolate Delights
A Collection of Chocolate Recipes
Cookbook Delights Series Book 3

Salads

Table of Contents

Page

Ambrosia Fruit Salad

This fruit salad is a welcome taste of sunshine during those longer months of winter when fresh fruits aren't as readily available.

Ingredients:

- 1 c. sour cream
- 2 c. whipped cream, lightly sweetened
- 1 can pineapple tidbits, drained (20 oz.)
- 2 cans mandarin oranges (11 oz. each,) drained
- 2 c. coconut, flaked, sweetened
- 2 c. miniature marshmallows
- 2 tsp. orange peel, fresh grated
- 1½ c. chocolate chips

Directions:

1. In large mixing bowl, combine sour cream and whipped cream.
2. Add remaining ingredients and gently fold until just combined.
3. Pour into serving dish; cover.
4. Refrigerate 2 hours before serving.

Candy Marshmallow Apple Salad

This is a sinfully rich salad that can actually double as a dessert. Everyone loves it, so make sure you have plenty, for seconds!

Ingredients:

- 6 chocolate/caramel/peanut candy bars, full size
- 7 Granny Smith apples, cored
- 1 pkg. cream cheese, room temperature (8 oz.)

1   jar marshmallow crème
1½ c. whipped cream (12 oz.)
      maraschino cherries, for garnish

Directions:

1. Cut candy bars and Granny Smith apples into bite-size pieces.
2. Cover and set aside.
3. In large mixing bowl, with electric mixer, whip cream cheese and marshmallow crème until smooth and creamy.
4. Fold in candy bars and apples.
5. Garnish with whipped cream and cherries.

Chocolate Candies Salad

This is an interesting sweet salad simply made with colorful types of chocolate and raisins.

Ingredients:

1 c. round chocolate-covered, plain candies
1 c. round peanut chocolate candies
1 c. chocolate-covered peanuts
1 c. chocolate-covered raisins
1 c. chocolate stars
1 c. malted milk balls

Directions:

1. In large serving bowl, combine all ingredients; toss lightly to mix.
2. You may add or delete anything that your chocolate-loving heart desires.
3. Note: If serving as a festive salad, use season colored chocolate-covered candies.

Clementine Chocolate Salad

Mandarin oranges, or Clementine's as they are known, combine for a great chocolate salad, and also it makes a great sweet salad to accompany a main dish or as a dessert.

Ingredients:

- 8 Clementine mandarin oranges
- ¾ c. almonds, flaked
- 10 fresh mint leaves, finely sliced
- 6 Tbs. caster sugar
- 4 Tbs. water
- 2 oz. quality cooking chocolate, shaved
    seeds from 1 vanilla pod

Directions:

1. Peel oranges, slice across thinly, and remove white matter.
2. Arrange on 4 plates; sprinkle with almonds and mint.
3. In small saucepan, bring sugar and water to boil.
4. Add vanilla seeds (see directions below).
5. Simmer until liquid becomes a light golden syrup. Try not to touch it too much at this stage.
6. Drizzle syrup over oranges.
7. Top with chocolate before serving.

Directions for removing seeds from vanilla pods:

1. Score the pods.
2. Scrape seeds out.
3. Add seeds to sugar and water mixture (above).
4. Place unwanted pods in a jar of sugar for delicious vanilla-flavored sugar.

Quick Vegetarian Mole

This is a surprising flavorful combination of flavors for a unique salad.

Ingredients:

2   Tbs. peanut oil
1   med. red onion, chopped
1   lg. red bell pepper, seeded, chopped
2   garlic cloves, crushed
2   tsp. ground coriander
1   tsp. ground cumin
½   tsp. ground cinnamon
1   lb. sweet potatoes, cut into cubes
1   lb. canned tomatoes, chopped (2 cups)
2   c. canned kidney beans, drained, rinsed
1-2 tsp. sweet chili sauce
1¼ c. water
1   oz. dark chocolate, grated
2   Tbs. fresh cilantro, chopped
      salt and freshly ground black pepper

Directions:

1. Heat oil in large saucepan over medium-high heat.
2. Sauté onion, pepper, garlic, and spices for 5 minutes, until onion is tender and spices are fragrant.
3. Add sweet potatoes, tomatoes, beans, chili sauce, and water; bring to a boil.
4. Cover, reduce heat to low; simmer 30 minutes.
5. During final 5 minutes, stir in chocolate and cilantro.
6. Taste, and adjust salt and pepper if necessary.
7. Ensure the potatoes are cooked through.
8. Serve hot with rice or corn bread.

Yields: 4 servings.

Strawberry Salad with Chocolate Dressing

Strawberries also combine with chocolate to make a unique salad. This one also adds blue cheese for a surprisingly rich combination of flavors.

Ingredients for dressing:

- ½ c. balsamic vinegar
- ½ c. superfine sugar
- 2 sq. dark chocolate (75% pure)

Ingredients for salad:

- 3½ oz. salad leaves, your favorite
- ½ cucumber
- 2 c. strawberries, halved
- ¼ c. Stilton cheese, with black pepper, crumbled

Directions for dressing:

1. Place balsamic vinegar in a saucepan, add sugar and dissolve over low heat.
2. Remove from heat.
3. Stir in chocolate.
4. Cool at room temperature.
5. Do not refrigerate or dressing will solidify.

Directions:

1. Divide lettuce between the plates.
2. Slice cucumber lengthwise, seed, and slice into half-moons.
3. Arrange cheese, cucumber, and strawberries on the lettuce.
4. Drizzle dressing on top.

Tomato Salad with Chocolate Dressing

This refreshing salad uses fresh tomatoes, poppy seeds, hard-boiled eggs topped off with a cinnamon and chocolate creamy dressing. You will surprise your guests with this salad, and it is very good.

Ingredients for chocolate dressing:

- 3 c. heavy whipping cream
- 8 Tbs. sugar
- 8 Tbs. cocoa powder
- 2 Tbs. cinnamon

Ingredients for salad:

- 6 lg. ripe tomatoes, chopped into ¼-inch pieces, drain
- ½ c. fresh basil
- ½ c. olive oil
- 1 Tbs. garlic powder
- 2 Tbs. poppy seeds
- 3 eggs, hard-boiled, cooled, chopped into ½-inch pieces

Directions:

1. In salad bowl, add tomatoes and basil.
2. In small bowl, combine olive oil, garlic powder, and poppy seeds.
3. Toss tomatoes, basil, oil with spices, and eggs together.
4. In medium bowl, with electric mixer on high speed, beat cream until thoroughly whipped.
5. Beat in sugar, cocoa powder, and cinnamon.
6. Pour cream over salad and mix gently.
7. Note: You may not need to add all the cream (just until it reaches a consistency that you like).
8. Chill and serve.
9. Garnish with sprinkles of cocoa powder and cinnamon, if desired.

Spiced Cocoa Chicken Salad

Cocoa and spices add a warm flavor to this colorful chicken salad.

Ingredients:

 2   Tbs. ground cumin
 2   Tbs. curry powder
 1   tsp. salt
 1   tsp. ground black pepper
 1½ Tbs. cocoa
 1   Tbs. canola oil
 6   boneless skinless chicken breasts (5 oz. each)
 ¾   c. olive oil
 ¼   c. apple cider vinegar
 8   c. salad greens
 1   lg. red bell pepper, cut into strips
 1   lg. orange bell pepper, cut into strips
 1   pt. cherry tomatoes, cut in half
 1   med. cucumber, sliced, cut in half
 12 radishes, sliced
 1½ c. couscous, cooked, cooled

Directions:

1. Preheat oven to 350 degrees F.
2. Lightly grease a baking sheet.
3. In small bowl, combine cumin, curry powder, salt, pepper, and cocoa; set aside.
4. Rub chicken breasts with oil.
5. Sprinkle 1 heaping teaspoon cocoa-curry mixture over each chicken breast; reserve remaining spice mix for dressing.
6. Place coated chicken on prepared baking sheet.
7. Bake 20 to 25 minutes, or until juices are clear.
8. Cool.
9. Slice into strips; set aside.

10. In medium bowl, combine remaining cocoa-curry spice mix, olive oil, and vinegar; blend well.
11. Cover; refrigerate until chilled.
12. To serve: Divide salad greens among 6 salad plates.
13. Arrange chicken slices, red peppers, orange peppers, cherry tomatoes, cucumbers, radishes, and cooled couscous on top of salad greens.
14. Serve immediately with dressing.

Cherry Pine Nut Salad

This salad uses the flavor of chocolate mint added with pine nuts to make a nutty, tangy, and sweet salad.

Ingredients for dressing:

2   Tbs. canola oil, divided
1   lime, juiced
1   pc. gingerroot, grated (1-inch piece)
20 chocolate mint leaves, finely chopped
    black pepper, to taste
    sea salt, to taste

Ingredients for salad:

½ c. pine nuts, roasted
1   c. fresh cherries, sliced
1   garlic clove, sliced
5   oz. mixed greens

Directions:

1. In small skillet, heat 1 teaspoon of oil over low heat.
2. Add garlic; cook until slightly browned, remove garlic from oil.
3. In salad bowl, toss salad ingredients together.
4. In small bowl, combine dressing ingredients; mix well.
5. Toss into the salad right before serving.

Chocolate Risotto Salad with Scallops

Scallops are one of my favorites, and combined with a creamy sauce, white chocolate, garlic, and arugula, this makes an excellent salad.

Ingredients:

    4 lg. sea scallops
    1 tsp. unsweetened cocoa powder
    1 sm. onion, finely diced
    1 c. Arborio rice
    3 c. chicken stock
    2 Tbs. butter
    ¼ c. heavy cream
    1 oz. white chocolate, roughly chopped
    1 lemon, zested, juiced
    2 Tbs. parsley, chopped
    1 garlic clove, finely chopped
    2 Tbs. olive oil
    1 c. arugula leaves, washed, dried
       salt and pepper, to taste

Directions:

1. Preheat a deep, large skillet over high heat.
2. Season scallops with salt and pepper, to taste.
3. Coat with cocoa powder.
4. When the pan is hot, add a little olive oil.
5. Sear scallops, turning once, 2 to 3 minutes per side.
6. Remove from pan; cover with tinfoil to keep warm.
7. Add butter to skillet; sauté onion until translucent.
8. Add rice; cook 1 minute, stirring to coat with butter.
9. Reduce heat to medium.
10. Add ⅓ cup stock at a time, stirring frequently to prevent rice from sticking.
11. Wait until most of the liquid is absorbed before adding more.

12. In small bowl, combine parsley, garlic, and lemon zest; set aside.
13. In small bowl, combine lemon juice, olive oil, and salt and pepper, to taste.
14. Once stock has been absorbed, add cream and taste the rice for doneness (it should be creamy and tender but not mushy).
15. Add more liquid and keep cooking if needed.
16. When done, season with salt and pepper to taste.
17. Add white chocolate, stirring to combine.
18. To serve, divide some of the risotto between two deep dinner plates.
19. Top each with two scallops.
20. Toss arugula with lemon vinaigrette and pile it onto the risotto next to the scallops.
21. Garnish scallops with lemon-garlic mixture.
22. Dust plate with a bit more cocoa powder.

Chocolate Salad

This is a unique salad, and great for company.

Ingredients:

5 slices white bread, heavy, chewy
3 kiwis, ripe, chilled
3 nectarines, ripe, chilled
3 tsp. cocoa powder
  fresh lemon juice

Directions:

1. In large salad bowl, cube bread and fruit.
2. Spray with fresh lemon.
3. Using a sieve or sifter, press cocoa powder on top.
4. Toss well and serve.

Balsamic Pear and Endive Salad

Our family loves pears and endives, and flavors added by using fresh cacao and cocoa powder to the dressing make for a unique taste.

Ingredients:

- 1 ripe pear, peeled, thinly sliced
- 2 sm. bunches of endive
- 4 oz. walnuts, toasted
- 1 oz. cacao nibs
- 4 Tbs. balsamic vinegar
- ½ tsp. unsweetened cocoa powder
- 3 Tbs. extra virgin olive oil
    lemon juice or vinegar
    salt and pepper, to taste
    bittersweet chocolate, for garnish

Directions:

1. In small saucepan, combine balsamic vinegar and cocoa powder.
2. Cook until reduced by half.
3. Cut off root end of endive bunches to separate the leaves.
4. In large salad bowl, lightly toss pear slices in a bit of lemon juice or white vinegar to keep from browning.
5. In small bowl, whisk together balsamic-cocoa mixture and olive oil; season to taste.
6. Just before serving, combine pear, endive, walnuts and vinaigrette.
7. Using a vegetable peeler, shave some bittersweet chocolate onto the salad and top with a sprinkle of cacao nibs.

Yields: 2 servings.

Spring Green Fruit Salad

My children love fruit salads, and enjoy the fruit of mandarin oranges, strawberries, blueberries with a surprise of white chocolate chips. Do enjoy!

Ingredients for dressing:

   ¼ c. champagne vinegar
   ⅓ c. reserved mandarin juice
   ¼ tsp. salt
   2 Tbs. sugar
   ¼ c. white chocolate chips
   2 Tbs. olive oil

Ingredients for salad:

   1 can mandarin oranges, drained, reserve juice (15 oz.)
   5 oz. spring greens, pre-washed
   2 c. strawberries
   ½ pt. blueberries

Directions:

   1. In large bowl, combine salad greens and fruit.
   2. In small saucepan, over medium-low heat, combine vinegar, reserved juice, salt, and sugar.
   3. Gently heat until sugar is dissolved.
   4. Remove from heat.
   5. Stir in white chocolate until melted; set aside to cool.
   6. Do not refrigerate, as white chocolate will set.
   7. Before serving, slowly whisk in olive oil.
   8. Pour over salad, or serve in a jar to pour on single servings yourself.

Spinach Salad with Chocolate Dressing

Fresh spinach and strawberries are topped off with a surprising raspberry chocolate dressing, which is excellent.

Ingredients for chocolate dressing:

- ⅓ c. olive oil
- ⅓ c. walnut oil
- ⅓ c. red raspberry white balsamic vinegar
- 2 Tbs. chocolate extract
  salt, to taste

Ingredients for salad:

- 11 oz. organic baby spinach
- 1 orange serrano pepper, seeded, rib removed, finely chopped
- 1½ pt. organic strawberries, washed, quartered
- 1 c. almonds, sliced

Directions for chocolate dressing:

1. In small bowl, combine all dressing ingredients.
2. Blend together until creamy in appearance.
3. Just before serving, pour into salad and toss.

Directions for salad:

1. In large salad bowl, combine salad ingredients; toss together.
2. Add chocolate dressing just prior to serving.

Did You Know? . . . .

Did you know the peak growing period for the average cocoa tree is 10 years?

Chocolate Delights
A Collection of Chocolate Recipes
Cookbook Delights Series Book 3

Side Dishes

Table of Contents

Mole-Style Baked Beans

Our family loves baked beans, and this actually has a warm taste with the combination of spices and chocolate to make a unique baked bean dish.

Ingredients:

1   lb. great northern beans, soaked overnight
10 c. cold water, divided
½ c. water, boiling
1   dried chipotle chile
3   Tbs. olive oil
1   med. onion, minced
4   slices bacon, finely chopped
¾ c. dark brown sugar
⅓ c. tomato paste
¼ c. dry red wine
⅛ tsp. nutmeg, freshly grated
⅛ tsp. cloves, ground
⅛ tsp. ground cumin
⅛ tsp. sweet paprika
⅛ tsp. chili powder
2   oz. unsweetened chocolate, chopped

Directions:

1. Drain and rinse the beans.
2. In large saucepan, cover beans with 6 cups water; bring to boil.
3. Reduce heat to low; cover, and simmer 1 hour until tender.
4. Meanwhile, soak chipotle in boiling water for 20 minutes until softened.
5. Drain chipotle.
6. Discard stem and seeds and mince.
7. Heat olive oil in a large saucepan.
8. Add onion.

9. Cook over moderate heat until softened, 2 to 3 minutes.
10. Add bacon; cook until softened, 2 to 3 minutes.
11. Stir in remaining 4 cups of water, chipotle, brown sugar, tomato paste, wine, nutmeg, cloves, cumin, paprika, and chili powder.
12. Drain beans; add to the saucepan.
13. Cover; simmer over low heat, 1 hour, or until sauce has thickened.
14. Stir in chocolate.
15. Season with salt and pepper.

Rice with Coconut and Chocolate

This side dish is slightly sweet and savory with the addition of coconut and chocolate for a unique side dish.

Ingredients:

¼ tsp. olive oil
1 onion, chopped
2 garlic cloves, minced
1 c. white rice
1 sq. unsweetened baking chocolate
1 c. coconut milk
water
salt, to taste

Directions:

1. In large skillet, sauté onion and garlic in oil.
2. Stir in rice.
3. Add coconut milk, water sufficient for cooking, salt, and baking chocolate.
4. Cook until rice is tender.
5. Serve with shrimp or fish.

Mexican Mole over Rice

This is a quick and easy mole that is unique with the flavors of the spices and sweetness of the chocolate, and it is very good.

Ingredients:

20 Roma tomatoes
8   jalapeño peppers
¼ c. walnuts, crushed
⅓ c. sesame seeds
¼ c. raisins
3   oz. bittersweet chocolate, melted
2   Tbs. garlic, minced
1   qt. vegetable stock
    rice, precooked

Directions:

1. Preheat oven to 500 degrees F. (broil)
2. Place tomatoes and jalapeño peppers on a baking sheet.
3. Broil 5 minutes, turning once, until they have begun to scorch on all sides.
4. Remove from oven.
5. Transfer peppers to a bowl; cover tightly with plastic wrap until cooled, about 15 minutes.
6. Slip skins off peppers, slit peppers open, and remove seeds.
7. In blender or food processor, blend tomatoes, peppers, walnuts, sesame seeds, raisins, chocolate, and garlic.
8. Lightly spray a skillet with cooking spray.
9. Heat over medium-high heat.
10. Add mixture to skillet; cook and stir until heated through.
11. Return mixture to blender.

12. Blend in enough vegetable stock to make a slightly thick sauce; blend well.
13. Serve over rice or other side dish.

White Chocolate Mashed Potatoes

My family loves mashed potatoes, and the addition of white chocolate adds creaminess and a very subtle flavor to these mashed potatoes.

Ingredients:

3   lb. potatoes, peeled
1½ oz. white chocolate, chopped
¾   tsp. salt
6   dashes hot red pepper sauce
1½ c. milk

Directions:

1. Place potatoes in large pot.
2. Cover with cool water to a depth of 2 inches.
3. Over high heat, bring to simmer.
4. Reduce heat; simmer 25 minutes, or until tender when pierced with a fork. Drain.
5. Return potatoes to pot.
6. Place over medium-low heat for 1 to 2 minutes to dry potatoes, stirring occasionally.
7. Add chocolate to the hot potatoes.
8. Stir until chocolate starts to melt.
9. Stir in salt and hot red pepper sauce.
10. With electric mixer on medium-low speed, mash potatoes slightly; pour in milk.
11. Continue mixing for 1 minute until creamy.
12. Serve at once.

Yields: 8 servings.

Roasted Vegetables

My family loves roasted vegetables, and this adds a very warm flavor with the warm spices, coffee, and chocolate to flavor the roasted vegetables.

Ingredients for hot chocolate Mexican spice blend:

    ½ c. chili powder
    ¼ c. paprika
    1 Tbs. ground cumin
    1 tsp. garlic powder
    1 tsp. red pepper flakes
    2 tsp. salt
    2 tsp. dried oregano leaves
    ½ c. toffee bits, crushed
    ½ c. cocoa
    1 Tbs. ground coffee beans

Ingredients for vegetables:

    2 Tbs. hot chocolate Mexican spice blend (see above)
    1 yellow pepper, cored, seeded
    1 red pepper, cored, seeded
    1 lg. red onion
    1 mango, firm but not hard, peeled
    1 yellow squash
    1 zucchini
    15 grape tomatoes
    1 lg. portobello mushroom, sliced lengthwise
    ¾ c. prepared vinaigrette dressing

Directions for hot chocolate Mexican spice blend:

1. In medium bowl, combine all ingredients; blend well.
2. Place in airtight container.
3. Note: Store in cool, dry place for up to 4 months.

Directions for vegetables:

1. Preheat oven to 450 degrees F.

2. Prepare hot chocolate Mexican spice blend; set aside.
3. Cut yellow pepper, red pepper, onion, mango, yellow squash, and zucchini into 1-inch pieces.
4. Place in large bowl; add tomatoes and mushroom.
5. Pour vinaigrette dressing and spice mix over vegetables; toss.
6. Spread vegetables in shallow baking pan.
7. Bake 20 to 30 minutes, or until vegetables are tender.

Mole de Arroz (Rice Mole)

This rice can also be made with vegetarian flavor, and it is delicious.

Ingredients:

3 c. chicken broth
2 med. onions, sliced
1½ c. rice, soaked
4 pasilla chiles, seeds, stems removed
3 cascabel chiles, seeds, stems removed
4 Tbs. canola oil
1 sq. baking chocolate
1 tsp. cumin
6 black peppercorns
4 garlic cloves, crushed
4 tomatillos, chopped
  salt, to taste

Directions:

1. In large saucepan, cook rice and onions in chicken broth until done, stirring occasionally.
2. In large skillet, fry chiles in oil.
3. Add cumin, peppercorns, garlic, chocolate, and tomatillos until chiles become soft; mix well.
4. Place in blender container; purée.
5. Return to skillet; add rice.
6. Cook several minutes; add salt, to taste.

Beans with Tomatoes and Chocolate

This recipe combines ground beef, beans, and tomatoes with chocolate to make a great flavorful combination for this side dish.

Ingredients:

12 oz. red beans, cooked
2 Tbs. canola oil
2 garlic cloves, diced
1 onion, diced
1 oz. unsweetened baking chocolate
7 oz. tomatoes, skinned, diced
14 oz. ground beef
    salt, to taste
    cumin, to taste
    dried malagueta or other chile peppers, to taste

Directions:

1. In large skillet, heat oil.
2. Sauté garlic and onion in oil.
3. Add ground beef.
4. Stir with wooden spoon until cooked through.
5. Add tomatoes, mix, and let cook covered for 5 minutes, stirring occasionally.
6. Add a little of the juice from the cooked red beans, just enough to cover.
7. Season with salt and spices, and let cook for 25 minutes.
8. Drain beans, reserving the water.
9. Add beans in the pan and cover with reserved water.
10. Cook over low heat for 20 minutes.
11. Adjust seasonings, adding salt, cumin, and chile peppers, to taste.
12. Serve with any meat dish and white rice.

Chocolate Delights
A Collection of Chocolate Recipes
Cookbook Delights Series Book 3

Soups

Table of Contents

Page

Cocoa Black Bean Soup

Our family loves black bean soup. This has delicious flavor with the combination of black beans, cocoa powder, and spices. It makes a hearty vegetarian meal that you can complete with a side salad, and your favorite dinner roll or bread.

Ingredients:

1	lb. dried black beans
10	c. water
1	tsp. salt
1	lg. green bell pepper, cored, halved
⅔	c. peanut oil or canola oil
1	lg. yellow onion, sliced
4	garlic cloves, minced
1	sm. hot green pepper, halved, seeded
3	tsp. salt, or to taste
½	tsp. black pepper, freshly ground
1½	Tbs. unsweetened cocoa powder
1	bay leaf
¼	tsp. whole cumin seed
1	tsp. sugar
2½	Tbs. red wine vinegar
2½	Tbs. olive oil

Directions:

1. Rinse black beans; soak overnight in water, salt, and large green bell pepper.
2. In large, heavy-bottomed, 6-quart soup pot, bring beans, soaking water, and pepper to a boil.
3. Reduce heat; simmer 45 minutes, or until tender.
4. Remove green pepper pieces and discard.
5. Heat peanut oil in a deep skillet or heavy saucepan.
6. Sauté onion, garlic, and hot green pepper until soft.
7. Remove 2½ cups of bean broth from the pot.

8. Add broth to the skillet; simmer 10 minutes.
9. Strain onions, garlic, and hot pepper from the broth; discard; add to the soup pot.
10. Add salt, pepper, cocoa, bay leaf, cumin, and sugar.
11. Bring to boil; simmer, covered, 1½ hours, or until soup thickens. You may need to add more water if too much liquid cooks away.
12. Before serving, add vinegar and olive oil; mix well.

Hot Fruit and Chocolate Soup

This is an easy-to-make soup, and is very tasty with the addition of your favorite fruits.

Ingredients:

4 c. fruit, cut into chunks, your choice
15 sq. dark chocolate (70% cocoa)
⅓ c. half and half cream
2 Tbs. butter
1 c. crème anglaise
¼ c. brown sugar

Directions:

1. Preheat oven to 500 degrees F. (broil)
2. Combine chopped fruit.
3. In double boiler or microwave oven, melt chocolate, cream, and butter until mixture is smooth.
4. Divide chocolate mixture among 4 to 6 ovenproof bowls.
5. Divide fruit, crème anglaise, and brown sugar equally into each bowl.
6. Place bowls on a baking sheet.
7. Broil 5 to 8 minutes.
8. Serve immediately.

Chocolate Chipotle Black Bean Soup

Chipotle and chocolate add great flavor to this black bean soup which can be made ahead. Serve with a side salad, and your favorite bread or roll.

Ingredients:

- 1 c. dried black beans
- 1 dried chipotle chile
- 2 Tbs. olive oil
- ½ tsp. cumin
- ½ onion, minced
- 2 whole cloves
- ¼ tsp. allspice
- ½ tsp. cinnamon
- 5 c. stock
- 1 oz. unsweetened baking chocolate
- 3 Tbs. tomato paste
- ½ tsp. salt, or to taste
- 1 c. peanut oil, for garnish
- 4 shallots, sliced paper-thin
  sour cream, for garnish

Directions:

1. Soak beans and chipotle covered in water overnight, or use the quick-soak method (cover with water, bring to boil; boil 5 minutes. Remove from heat and let sit, covered, 1 hour).
2. Drain beans and chipotle.
3. Heat olive oil in a large soup pot.
4. Add cumin and onions; stir 3 minutes.
5. Add cloves, allspice, cinnamon, stock, chocolate, and soaked beans and chile.
6. Bring to boil; reduce heat, simmer 1 to 1½ hours, or until beans are tender.
7. Remove 2 cups of soup and the chipotle.

8. Purée in blender, return to pot.
9. Stir in tomato paste; mix well. Add salt, to taste.
10. In small skillet, heat peanut oil.
11. Add shallots; sauté 2 to 3 minutes, until crispy.
12. Drain into a sieve reserving oil, or remove them quickly with a slotted spoon onto paper towels.
13. Serve with a dollop of sour cream, and a sprinkle of crispy shallots.
14. Note: The used oil is great for instant flavor in your favorite stir-fry.

Cinnamon Chocolate Soup

This is a delicious dessert soup made with cinnamon and cocoa.

Ingredients:

1 c. milk
½ c. heavy whipping cream
2 Tbs. unsweetened cocoa powder
2 Tbs. white sugar
¼ tsp. vanilla extract
¼ tsp. ground cinnamon
    miniature marshmallows
    graham cracker bears

Directions:

1. In medium saucepan, heat all but 2 tablespoons of the milk and cream; do not boil.
2. In soup bowl, mix cocoa, sugar, vanilla, cinnamon, and reserved milk and cream.
3. Pour cocoa mixture into hot milk mixture; blend well. Return mixture to bowl.
4. Garnish with miniature marshmallows or graham cracker bears.

Spiced Chocolate Soup

Try this delicious spicy chocolate soup with caramel whipped cream.

Ingredients:

8   Tbs. sugar, divided
1   Tbs. butter, unsalted
⅛   tsp. salt
1½ c. heavy cream, divided
7   oz. semi or bittersweet chocolate, finely chopped
2½ c. milk
1   Tbs. peppercorns, crushed

Directions:

1. Warm a small saucepan over medium-low heat.
2. Sprinkle 5 tablespoons of sugar into the saucepan, a little at a time; adding more as the sugar melts.
3. When the sugar has turned a deep golden brown, add butter, salt and 1 cup of cream.
4. Bring to boil, stirring to dissolve the caramel.
5. Refrigerate at least 6 hours or preferably overnight.
6. Put cooled cream mixture into a large mixing bowl.
7. With electric mixer, whip until medium peaks form; refrigerate.
8. Put the chocolate in a medium bowl.
9. In medium saucepan, bring milk, remaining cream, and remaining sugar to boil.
10. Add peppercorn and remove from heat.
11. Cover and let infuse for 15 minutes.
12. Strain liquid through a fine-mesh sieve into a saucepan and bring to boil.
13. Pour over the chocolate and stir until the chocolate has melted, and mixture is smooth.
14. Strain through a fine-mesh sieve into a bowl.
15. Ladle soup into warm soup bowls.

16. Serve topped with a dollop of the caramel whipped cream.

Yields: 4 servings.

Hot Chocolate Soup

This is another unique soup that you can try as an entrée to surprise your guests with a chocolate soup.

Ingredients:

½ c. sugar
5 Tbs. flour
2 Tbs. cocoa
4 c. milk
½ tsp. vanilla extract
⅛ tsp. salt
3 slices of bread
¼ c. butter

Directions:

1. Preheat oven to 500 degrees F. (broil)
2. In small, heatproof dish, combine sugar, flour and cocoa.
3. Put under broiler and brown, stirring frequently.
4. Remove from heat.
5. Stir in a little milk until creamy; cool.
6. In small saucepan, heat remaining milk to boiling point.
7. Gradually stir in cocoa mixture; bring to boil.
8. Stir in vanilla and salt.
9. Cube the bread.
10. In small skillet, heat butter.
11. Fry bread cubes until golden brown.
12. Serve with hot soup.

Hazelnut Chocolate Soup

This dessert soup is a unique beginning course for a sweet entrée.

Ingredients:

   4 c. half and half cream
   6 oz. semi-sweet or bittersweet chocolate
   ½ c. sugar
   4 egg yolks, at room temperature
   ⅓ c. crème de cacao
   3 Tbs. hazelnut liqueur
   ½ c. whipping cream, lightly whipped
   ½ c. hazelnuts, chopped, toasted
   ½ c. chocolate sprinkles or curls

Directions:

   1. In medium saucepan, combine cream, chocolate, and sugar.
   2. Place over medium-low heat, stirring frequently until chocolate melts.
   3. Beat egg yolks in a small bowl.
   4. Whisk in ½ cup of chocolate mixture.
   5. Whisk egg mixture into soup; stirring frequently for 5 minutes, or until soup thickens slightly.
   6. Remove from heat; stir in the liqueurs.
   7. To serve hot, ladle into warmed bowls, add a dollop of whipped cream, sprinkle with hazelnuts and chocolate sprinkles, and serve immediately.
   8. To serve cold, pour into an airtight container; refrigerate 2 hours until chilled.
   9. Remove from refrigerator 20 minutes before serving.
   10. Ladle into chilled bowls; garnish as for hot soup.
   11. Note: This may be kept in an airtight container in the refrigerator for up to 5 days.
   12. Slowly reheat before garnishing and serving.

Yields: 6 servings.

Mexican Chocolate Soup

Try this spicy Mexican chocolate soup for a change of pace.

Ingredients:

½ onion, diced
1 carrot, diced
2 celery stalks, diced
1 med. zucchini, diced
1 green bell pepper, diced
1 jalapeño pepper, diced
2 Tbs. canola oil
1 Tbs. tequila, more if desired
2 Tbs. cocoa
1 Tbs. flour
½ tsp. ground cinnamon
1 qt. chicken broth
½ c. fresh cilantro, chopped
½ tsp. salt
½ tsp. pepper

Directions:

1. In large Dutch oven, sauté vegetables in oil until crisp-tender.
2. Add tequila; remove from heat.
3. In small bowl, combine cocoa, flour, and cinnamon; stir into vegetable mixture.
4. Add broth.
5. Over medium-high heat, bring to boil, stirring constantly.
6. Reduce heat; simmer, stirring occasionally, 5 to 10 minutes, or until tender.
7. Stir in cilantro, salt, and pepper.

Yields: 6 cups.

Chocolate Soup with Breadsticks

Try this version of chocolate soup that is served with glazed bread sticks.

Ingredients for soup:

> 6 sq. chocolate, broken into small pieces
> 1 qt. water
> 1 qt. milk
> 1 cinnamon stick
> 1 c. sugar
> 2 egg yolks
> 1 c. cream, divided

Ingredients for breadsticks:

> bread, cut into thin strips
> butter
> powdered sugar

Directions for breadsticks:

1. Preheat oven to 250 degrees F.
2. Spread butter on bread strips; sift sugar over top.
3. Place on baking sheet.
4. Bake until crisp and glazed.

Directions for soup:

1. Place chocolate in large saucepan, cover with water.
2. Over low heat, melt chocolate; bring to boil.
3. In large saucepan, heat milk.
4. Add cinnamon stick and sugar.
5. When chocolate is boiling, add to milk mixture.
6. In large bowl, whisk yolks and ½ cup cream together.
7. Strain chocolate mixture over egg yolk mixture; cool in refrigerator.
8. Just before serving, whip remaining cream and stir into the soup. Serve with breadsticks.

Turkey and Black Bean Soup

This soup is a rich-tasting broth that is full of turkey, black beans, and bacon with the surprising ingredient of cocoa.

Ingredients:

¼ lb. bacon, sliced, cut crosswise into ¼-inch strips
1 onion, chopped
1 Tbs. chili powder
½ tsp. unsweetened cocoa powder
¼ tsp. hot sauce
2 tsp. dried oregano
2 tsp. salt
¼ tsp. fresh ground black pepper
1 can tomatoes, crushed (15 oz.)
4 c. low-sodium chicken broth or homemade
1 can black beans, drained, rinsed (15 oz.)
1 lb. turkey, deli-style, cooked, cut into ½ x ½ x ¼-inch slices
1 pkg. spinach, stems removed, washed, cut into 1-inch strips (10 oz.)

Directions:

1. In large stainless steel pot, cook bacon until crisp.
2. Remove with slotted spoon; drain on paper towels. Pour off all but 1 tablespoon of fat from the pot.
3. Reduce heat to medium-low; add onion, cook 5 minutes, or until translucent, stir frequently.
4. Stir in chili powder, cocoa, hot sauce, oregano, salt, pepper, tomatoes, and broth; bring to boil.
5. Reduce heat; simmer 15 minutes.
6. Add beans and turkey to the pot; simmer 5 minutes.
7. Stir in spinach and bacon.
8. Cook 1 minutes, or until spinach just wilts.
9. Note: Use smoked turkey in place of plain.
10. Substitute 1⅔ cups drained and rinsed kidney, pinto, or cannellini beans for the black beans.

Chipotle Black Bean Soup

The smoky, spicy almost chocolate-like flavor of this soup comes from chipotle chilies. The unsweetened cocoa, adds warmth to the unique flavor of this soup. Serve with cornbread or your favorite bread.

Ingredients:

⅛ c. olive oil
1 c. red onion, chopped
1 med. red bell pepper, seeded, chopped
1 med. green bell pepper, seeded, chopped
2 garlic cloves, minced
1 Tbs. dried oregano, or 3 Tbs. fresh
1 Tbs. ground cumin
3 chipotle chilies, canned, reserve sauce, chopped
⅛ c. adobo sauce from canned chipotle peppers
12 c. water
1 bay leaf
2 c. black beans, dry, rinsed
1 Tbs. unsweetened cocoa powder
¾ c. orange juice
½ c. fresh cilantro, minced
6 scallions, thinly sliced
   sea salt, to taste

Directions:

1. Soak beans overnight or 8 hours prior to cooking.
2. In large soup pot, heat oil over medium-high heat.
3. Add onion, red and green peppers, and garlic; sauté until onion is translucent.
4. Reduce heat to medium-low.
5. Add oregano, cumin, chipotle chilies, and adobo sauce; sauté 1 minute.
6. Add cold water, bay leaf, and beans.
7. Bring soup to boil; reduce heat to simmer.
8. Cook, uncovered, 1½ to 2 hours, or until beans are tender.

9. Stir in cocoa powder, orange juice, cilantro, scallions, and salt; simmer 5 more minutes.

Chocolate Rose Petal Soup

Try this unique chocolate rose petal soup. You may garnish with hazelnuts and pound cake croutons if desired.

Ingredients:

    4 oz. dark milk chocolate (41% cocoa)
    4 oz. dark chocolate (58.5% cocoa)
    1 c. half and half cream
    ½ tsp. vanilla extract
    2 organic, pesticide-free, edible roses or the equivalent amount in rose petals
    ½ c. fresh strawberries, sliced in small wedges
    4 fresh mint leaves, more if desired

Directions:

1. Chop chocolate into small slivers; set aside.
2. In small saucepan, stirring occasionally, bring cream to simmer.
3. Remove from heat; add chocolate. Let sit 5 minutes. After 5 minutes, stir in what hasn't melted.
4. Stir in vanilla.
5. Note: The soup should be smooth and a little thick. If the chocolate soup is too rich or too thick for your taste, to add a little more cream or water until desired consistency.
6. Ladle ½ cup soup into small, flat bowls.
7. Remove rose petals from stems.
8. Arrange the individual petals into the shape of a flower on top of the soup.
9. Do 1 to 2 overlapping layers to give dimension.
10. Top center of rose petals with a cluster of strawberries.
11. Garnish with a sprinkling of mint leaves.

Roasted Squash Soup

Try this delicious fall soup with the added delight of drizzled cream infused with cocoa beans.

Ingredients for soup:

2   Tbs. olive oil
1   med. yellow onion, chopped
1¾ lb. butternut squash, peeled, oven roasted
4   c. chicken or vegetable broth, more if desired
¼   c. dry sherry (optional)
1   Tbs. agave nectar (optional)
1   Tbs. sage leaves, chopped
½   tsp. salt
⅛   tsp. freshly ground white pepper, or to taste

Ingredients for cocoa crème:

3   Tbs. cocoa nibs, crushed
2   Tbs. soymilk
2   Tbs. soy creamer
6   Tbs. tofu sour cream

Directions:

1. In large soup pot, heat oil over medium-high heat.
2. Sauté onions until tender and a little browned.
3. Add squash, broth, sherry, agave, sage, salt, and pepper; simmer.
4. Mix cocoa nibs with soymilk in a small pitcher; microwave on medium for 1 minute, or bring to simmer in a small saucepan, to infuse the milk with the cocoa flavor.
5. In large bowl, combine creamer and tofu sour cream.
6. Mix in cocoa-milk mixture.
7. Purée with a hand-held blender until very smooth.
8. Taste; adjust salt and pepper if necessary.
9. Divide between 6 soup bowls.
10. Drizzle cocoa crème over each bowl and serve.

Chocolate Soup with Cinnamon Apples

This is a delicious chocolate soup served with cinnamon apples, bread cubes, and whipped cream.

Ingredients:

2 Tbs. butter
1 c. apples, peeled, chopped in fine cubes
¾ c. sugar, divided
1 tsp. ground cinnamon
2 cinnamon sticks, broken in pieces
2 c. water
8 oz. chocolate (67% cocoa) cut in small pieces
1 c. cream
2 slices of bread, cut in cubes

Directions:

1. In large saucepan, melt butter.
2. Add apples, 5 teaspoons sugar, and ground cinnamon; mix well.
3. Over medium heat, cook 3 minutes. The apples should be still crispy.
4. In small saucepan, over low heat, add ⅓ cup sugar, stirring constantly.
5. Add cinnamon sticks; let sugar caramelize until it is a dark color.
6. Slowly add water; boil 3 minutes.
7. Remove cinnamon sticks.
8. Whisk in chocolate pieces; boil 1 minute.
9. In small bowl, whisk cream with remaining sugar until soft peaks forms.
10. Refrigerate until cold.
11. Divide apple mixture into serving bowls.
12. Pour equal amounts of chocolate mixture over top.
13. Place bread cubes equally on each serving.
14. Top with whipped cream; sprinkle with cinnamon.

Baked Chocolate Soup

Try this delicious baked chocolate soup for a change of pace.

Ingredients:

8   oz. couverture semi-sweet chocolate, room temperature, cut into ¼-inch flakes
3   c. milk, scalded
6   bananas, ripe but not mushy, peeled, quartered
1   tsp. ground cinnamon
½ c. dark rum
¾ c. sugar, divided
4   Tbs. butter, unsalted
½ c. egg whites
1¼ c. powdered sugar

Directions:

1. Place chocolate in bowl; pour hot milk over top. Blend until smooth.
2. Cut banana quarters crosswise into ½-inch pieces.
3. Place in bowl, toss with cinnamon, and pour in rum.
4. In heavy, 10-inch frying pan over high heat; pour in sugar and cook until caramel brown; swirl in butter.
5. When melted, scrape in bananas and rum.
6. Sauté until bananas are softened and caramelized. Add a few drops of rum to melt caramel if needed.
7. Spread bananas evenly on bottom of soup tureen.
8. Spoon chocolate over bananas to cover ¼-inch thick, leaving ¼-inch to rim of container.
9. Cover; refrigerate 1 hour.
10. Preheat oven to 350 degrees F.
11. Place tureen in baking pan; pour boiling water around it.
12. In small bowl, with electric mixer, beat egg whites until foamy; gradually sift in ½ cup sugar. When whites form stiff peaks, fold in remaining sugar.
13. Scrape into a piping bag and swirl 1½ inches of meringue on the top of each dessert.
14. Remove tureen from water bath; set on baking sheet.
15. Bake 6 to 8 minutes, or until meringue is light brown.

Chocolate Delights
A Collection of Chocolate Recipes
Cookbook Delights Series Book 3

Wines and Spirits

Table of Contents

Page

About Cooking with Alcohol

Some recipes in this cookbook contain, among other ingredients, liquors. It is for the purpose of obtaining desired flavor and achieving culinary appreciation and not to be abused in any way. In cooking and baking, alcohol evaporates and only the flavor may be enjoyed. When mixed in cold, however, such as in desserts, caution must be exercised. These recipes are intended for people who may consume small amounts of alcohol in a responsible and safe manner.

I live in Washington State and we are proud of our wine production. Washington State is rapidly gaining prestige as a premier wine producer. Do enjoy the art of wine tasting and enjoy the completeness and uniqueness of each wine. It is an art to enjoy and savor in moderation.

If consumption of even small amounts of alcoholic ingredients presents a problem, in whatever form, please substitute coffee flavor syrups, found in coffee sections of supermarkets. For example, instead of Southern Comfort liqueur, substitute with Irish Cream or Amaretto Syrup.

Karen Jean Matsko Hood

Almond Hot Chocolate

This is a delicious version of hot chocolate with rum.

Ingredients:

   1 oz. rum (dark)
   1 Tbs. Orgeat syrup
   6 oz. hot chocolate

Directions:

   1. Mix in pousse cafe glass.

Choco Colada

This is a festive mix of flavors to enjoy. Nobody said we can't replace pineapple with chocolate.

Ingredients:

½ oz. cream
¾ oz. coconut cream
¾ oz. chocolate syrup
¼ oz. coffee liqueur
½ oz. rum (white)
½ oz. rum (dark)

Directions:

1. In shaker jar or small pitcher, combine all ingredients.
2. Mix well.
3. Serve in a margarita glass.
4. Top with chocolate shavings.

Chocolate Almond

This can also be made with light crème de cacao, but many prefer it dark.

Ingredients:

⅓ oz. amaretto
⅓ oz. dark crème de cacao
⅓ oz. Irish cream

Directions:

1. In small glass, add ingredients in the order listed.
2. Mix well.

Chocolate Black Russian

This is a very festive and creamy drink to enjoy on a hot summer evening.

Ingredients:

> 1 oz. coffee-flavored liqueur
> ½ oz. vodka
> 5 oz. chocolate ice cream

Directions:

1. Combine all ingredients in an electric blender.
2. Blend at low speed for a short length of time.
3. Pour into a chilled champagne flute and serve.

Chocolate-Covered Cherry

This chocolate milk with vodka and amaretto is beautifully colored by grenadine.

Ingredients:

> 1 oz. amaretto
> ½ oz. vodka
> 2 oz. chocolate milk
> 1 tsp. grenadine
> light cream to taste (optional)

Directions:

1. In a shaker jar half filled with ice cubes, combine all ingredients.
2. Shake well.
3. Strain into a cocktail glass.

Tie Me Up In Silk

You will enjoy this Irish cream drink with chocolate and rum.

Ingredients:

> 2 oz. Irish cream
> 1 oz. cream
> ½ oz. chocolate (melted)
> ½ oz. rum

Directions:

1. Pour the Irish cream, cream, and rum into an Irish coffee mug, and stir gently.
2. Drizzle melted chocolate over the top and serve.

White Chocolate Martini

This is another martini variation to enjoy.

Ingredients:

> 3 oz. vodka
> 1½ oz. chocolate liqueur (white)

Directions:

1. Shake ingredients with ice and strain into a martini glass.
2. Garnish with shaved chocolate.

Did You Know? . . . .

Did you know if it isn't chocolate, it just isn't anything?

Chocolate-Covered Strawberry

This is a bit different for a chocolate drink that I am certain you will enjoy.

Ingredients:

> 1 oz. tequila rose
> 1 oz. crème de cacao
> 1 oz. milk

Directions:

> 1. In a shaker jar, shake ingredients together with moderate ice.
> 2. Strain into a cocktail glass and serve.

Chocolate Cow

Chocolate and Kahlúa combine to make a tasty drink.

Ingredients:

> 1 shot chocolate liqueur
> 1 shot Kahlúa
> cream, to taste

Directions:

> 1. Pour all ingredients over ice in a cocktail glass.

Did You Know? . . . .

Did you know that chocoholics believe chocolate is its own food group?

Chocolate Crème Amaretto

Another enjoyable version of chocolate milk, this one is made with amaretto and crème de cacao.

Ingredients:

  1 oz. amaretto
  1 oz. crème de cacao
  4 oz. milk

Directions:

  1. Pour ingredients over ice in a highball glass.
  2. Stir and serve.

Chocolate Martini

This is called a martini but is nothing like the classic martini, and makes an excellent dessert drink.

Ingredients:

  1½ shots chocolate liqueur
  1½ shots crème de cacao
  ½ shot vodka
  2   shots heavy cream

Directions:

  1. Add all ingredients to a cocktail mixer and shake well.
  2. Pour into a chilled martini glass dusted with chocolate powder.

Chocolate Milk

This is another version of chocolate milk, this one with chocolate liqueur and amaretto.

Ingredients:

½ shot chocolate liqueur
½ shot milk
1 dash amaretto

Directions:

1. Put milk in the bottom of a glass, pour the liqueur on top, and add the dash of amaretto.
2. Do not mix.

Chocolate Peppermint Patty

I have always enjoyed chocolate with peppermint, and this hot chocolate drink is no exception.

Ingredients:

½ c. hot chocolate
1 shot peppermint liqueur
1 shot chocolate liqueur
sweetened whipped cream

Directions:

1. Pour hot chocolate into a brandy snifter.
2. Add 1 shot peppermint liqueur.
3. Add 1 shot chocolate liqueur.
4. Stir.
5. Top with whipped cream.

Chocolate Monkey

This recipe is a rich dessert drink with a wonderful blend of chocolate liqueurs and bananas.

Ingredients:

1 shot banana liqueur
2 shots crème de cacao
2 scoops chocolate ice cream
1 oz. chocolate syrup
4 oz. chocolate milk
1 c. whipped cream
1 cherry
1 piece banana

Directions:

1. In small pitcher, blend liqueurs with ice cream, milk, and syrup.
2. Pour into parfait glass, top with whipped cream, and garnish with banana and cherry.

Chocolate Shock

Cinnamon in the aftershock and chocolate make a pleasing taste combination.

Ingredients:

8 oz. hot chocolate
1 shot aftershock

Directions:

1. Add 1 shot of aftershock to 8-ounce cup of hot chocolate and enjoy.

Chocolate Snow Bear

This chocolate amaretto with ice cream is wonderful.

Ingredients:

  1 oz. amaretto
  1 oz. crème de cacao
  5 oz. vanilla ice cream (French)
  ¼ oz. chocolate syrup
  2 dashes vanilla extract

Directions:

  1. Combine all ingredients in electric blender and blend at low speed for a short length of time.
  2. Pour into a chilled champagne flute and serve.

Chocolate Soldier

This is another version of spiced chocolate milk, this one with rum.

Ingredients:

  1½ oz. chocolate liqueur
  1½ oz. spiced rum
  6 oz. milk
     chocolate syrup (optional)

Directions:

  1. Add all ingredients to a frosted beer mug.
  2. Also add chocolate syrup, if desired.
  3. Optional: A good chocolate syrup recipe can be found on page 185 of this cookbook.

Cioccolato e Cocco Rum

Coconut rum with cream and chocolate makes a very good drink.

Ingredients:

>   3 oz. milk
>   ¾ oz. coconut rum
>   ¾ oz. cream of coconut
>   ¾ oz. heavy cream
>   ¾ oz. crème de cacao

Directions:

1. In small pitcher, mix all ingredients thoroughly.
2. Pour into a glass.

Mint Chocolate Cream

Crème de cacao and crème de menthe combine to make an exciting drink for your guests to enjoy.

Ingredients:

>   ¾ oz. vodka
>   ¾ oz. crème de cacao
>   ¾ oz. crème de menthe
>   4 oz. milk
>   whipped cream, for garnish

Directions:

1. Pour vodka, crème de cacao, crème de menthe in a highball glass filled with ice.
2. Fill the rest of the glass with milk.
3. Top with whipped cream, and serve.

Hazelnut Truffles Cocktail

Chocolate and hazelnut is a match made in heaven. These flavors combine for an elegant ending to your special dinner party.

Ingredients:

6 oz. Frangelico (¾ c.)
6 oz. Godiva liqueur (¾ c.)
   milk chocolate or semi-sweet chocolate, shaved

Directions:

1. Dip the edges of 4 martini glasses in the liqueurs and rim them with shaved chocolate.
2. In small spouted or lipped-rim saucepan, combine the Frangelico and Godiva liqueurs.
3. Heat over medium to high heat until warm but not hot.
4. Pour into the chocolate-rimmed martini glasses, being careful not to disturb the chocolate, and serve.
5. Note: If spouted or lipped-rim pan is not available, pour the warm liqueur into the martini glasses through a funnel.

Yields: 4 servings.

Portuguese Licoro

This homemade liqueur recipe originates from the island of St. Michael in the Azores.

Ingredients:

1   qt. whiskey
½   lemon
4½ c. sugar

1   qt. milk
6   squares unsweetened chocolate (1 oz. ea.)
2   vanilla beans

Directions:

1. In a gallon container, combine whiskey, lemon half, sugar, milk, chocolate squares, and vanilla beans.
2. Keep at room temperature for 10 days, stirring once a day.
3. After 10 days, remove the lemon half, remaining chocolate squares, and vanilla beans.
4. Insert a coffee filter into a large funnel.
5. Pour the liquid through the filter into a gallon jug.
6. Change filter as needed (a clear yellow solution should result).
7. If your solution is not clear, then refilter until clear.
8. This liqueur can be stored in a sealed bottle at room temperature.

Jamaica Hop

This is another coffee brandy with cream, but with white chocolate. I think you will enjoy this.

Ingredients:

1 oz. coffee brandy
1 oz. white crème de cacao
1 oz. light cream
   ice cubes

Directions:

1. In shaker jar, shake all ingredients with ice.
2. Strain into a cocktail glass, and serve.

Creamy Grasshopper

White chocolate with ice cream and green mint is a delicious and festive drink to serve.

Ingredients:

¾ oz. white crème de cacao
¾ oz. green crème de menthe
2 scoops vanilla ice cream

Directions:

1. In blender, combine all ingredients; blend until smooth.
2. Drink should have a thick, shake-like consistency.

Chocolate Creamed Coffee Liqueur

This sweetened whipped cream is enhanced with the rich flavor of coffee-flavored liqueur and rum.

Ingredients:

2 c. heavy cream, well chilled
⅓ c. powdered sugar
3 Tbs. unsweetened cocoa
2 Tbs. coffee-flavored liqueur
2 Tbs. dark Jamaican rum

Directions:

1. In large bowl, place cream, powdered sugar, and cocoa.
2. Using wire whisk, stir just enough to blend; sugar and cocoa will not dissolve completely.
3. Cover; chill in refrigerator 1 hour.
4. Using an electric mixer, whip on medium speed with chilled beaters until cream begins to thicken.

5. Add liqueur and beat until cream falls in soft mounds when beaters are lifted.
6. Remove from mixer bowl.
7. Using a hand-held balloon whisk, whip until cream thickens, is smooth, and holds its shape.
8. Do not beat, as this will cause cream to become grainy.

Milky Way Martini

This martini tastes just like a Milky Way candy bar, so be careful not to consume too many!

Ingredients:

2 oz. vanilla vodka
2 oz. chocolate liqueur
1 oz. Irish cream

Directions:

1. In small pitcher, combine all ingredients; mix well.
2. Serve in martini glass without ice.

White Chocolate Russian

If you prefer white chocolate, you will enjoy this drink.

Ingredients:

1 jigger vodka
1 oz. white crème de cacao
1 oz. cream
ice cubes

Directions:

1. In small pitcher or shaker jar, combine all ingredients; mix well.
2. Serve over ice.

Mint Chocolate Ice Cream

This mint chocolate ice cream taste is a favorite of many guests.

Ingredients:

¾ oz. vodka
¾ oz. créme de cacao
¾ oz. créme de menthe
4 oz. milk
   whipped cream, for garnish

Directions:

1. Pour liquors into a highball glass filled with ice.
2. Fill the rest of the glass with milk.
3. Top with whipped cream and serve.

Orange Bomb

Chocolate, orange, and cream makes this drink delightful. Enjoy!

Ingredients:

1 oz. mandarin orange liqueur
½ oz. chocolate liqueur
½ oz. Irish cream
½ oz. half and half cream
   chocolate sprinkles

Directions:

1. In shaker jar, combine all ingredients; shake well.
2. Pour into glasses.
3. Garnish with chocolate sprinkles.

Chocolate Festival Information

Please check your local Chamber of Commerce or Visitor's Information Bureau for chocolate festivals in your area.

Long Grove Annual Chocolate Festival
Long Grove Chamber of Commerce
3110 RFD, Long Grove, IL 60047-9635
Phone: (847) 634-9440 | Fax: (847) 634-9408
Website: http://www.longgrove.net

Scottsdale Fine Art and Chocolate Festival
Scottsdale Chamber of Commerce
7343 Scottsdale Mall, Scottsdale, AZ 85251-4498
Phone: (480) 945-8481 | Toll-free: (800) 877-1117
Fax: (480) 947-4523

Valentine Pro/Am Chocolate Festival
Logan Chamber Of Commerce
160 N Main Street, Logan, UT 84321-4541
Phone: (435) 752-2161

Glendale Chocolate Affaire
Glendale Chamber of Commerce
7105 N. 59th Avenue, P.O. Box 249, Glendale, AZ 85311
Phone: 623 937-4754 | Toll-free: (800) 437-8669
Fax: (623) 937-3333

Maryland Chocolate Festival
Baltimore City Chamber
3 W. Baltimore, Baltimore, MD 21202
Phone: (410) 837-7101 | Fax: (410) 284-9864

The Chocolate Festival
Galesburg Commerce Center
292 East Simmons Street, Galesburg, Illinois 61401
Phone: (309) 343-1194 | Fax: (309) 343-1195
Email: chamber@galesburg.org

Firehouse Art Center Chocolate Festival
Norman Convention & Visitors Bureau
224 W. Gray, Suite 104, Norman, OK 73069
Toll Free: (800) 767-7260 | Phone: (405) 366-8095

Chocolate Associations and Commissions

Chocolate Manufacturers Association (CMA):
Represents 90% of chocolate processed in USA since 1923.
8320 Old Courthouse Road
Suite 300, Vienna, VA 22182
Phone: (703) 790-5011
Fax: (703) 790-5752
Email: carly.zoerb@chocolateusa.org

The Biscuit, Cake, Chocolate and Confectionery Alliance:
A trade association that represents one of the UK food industry's largest sectors.
Website: www.bccca.org.uk

International Office of Cocoa/Chocolate/Sugar Confectionery: Technical and scientific aspects of cocoa, chocolate candy, and confectionery industry.
Website: www.candy.net.au/IOCCC/main.htm

Pennsylvania Manufacturing Confectioners' Assoc.
An international trade association made up of confectionery manufacturers and supplier companies in related industries.
Website: www.pmca.com

Germany's Data Sweet Company offers a suite of services for the confectionery and chocolate industry. For industry conferences and seminar calendars, web design services, presentation design services, and listings of industry trade journals and publications.
Website: www.datasweet.com

International Cocoa Association (ICCO)
Statistics on the cocoa bean and chocolate. Publications on line. Industry and consumer related links.
Website: www.icco.org/questions/process.htm

The Manufacturing Confectioner
Business, marketing, and production journal of confectionery and chocolate industry worldwide.
Website: www.gomc.com

U.S. and Metric Measurement Charts

Here are some measurement equivalents to help you with exchanges. There was a time when many people thought the entire world would convert to the metric scale. While most of the world has, America still has not. Metric conversions in cooking are vitally important to preparing a tasty recipe. Here are simple conversion tables that should come in handy.

U.S. Measurement Equivalents

a few grains/pinch/dash (dry) = less than ⅛ teaspoon
a dash (liquid) = a few drops
3 teaspoons = 1 tablespoon
½ tablespoon = 1½ teaspoons
1 tablespoon = 3 teaspoons
2 tablespoons = 1 fluid ounce
4 tablespoons = ¼ cup
5⅓ tablespoons = ⅓ cup
8 tablespoons = ½ cup
8 tablespoons = 4 fluid ounces
10⅔ tablespoons = ⅔ cup
12 tablespoons = ¾ cup
16 tablespoons = 1 cup
16 tablespoons = 8 fluid ounces
⅛ cup = 2 tablespoons
¼ cup = 4 tablespoons
¼ cup = 2 fluid ounces
⅓ cup = 5 tablespoons plus 1 teaspoon
½ cup = 8 tablespoons
1 cup = 16 tablespoons
1 cup = 8 fluid ounces
1 cup = ½ pint
2 cups = 1 pint
2 pints = 1 quart
4 quarts (liquid) = 1 gallon
8 quarts (dry) = 1 peck
4 pecks (dry) = 1 bushel
1 kilogram = approximately 2 pounds
1 liter=approximately 4 cups or 1quart

Approximate Metric Equivalents by Volume

U.S.	Metric
¼ cup =	60 milliliters
½ cup =	120 milliliters
1 cup =	230 milliliters
1¼ cups =	300 milliliters
1½ cups =	360 milliliters
2 cups =	460 milliliters
2½ cups =	600 milliliters
3 cups =	700 milliliters
4 cups (1 quart) =	.95 liter
1.06 quarts =	1 liter
4 quarts (1 gallon) =	3.8 liters

Approximate Metric Equivalents by Weight

U.S.	Metric
¼ ounce =	7 grams
½ ounce =	14 grams
1 ounce =	28 grams
1¼ ounces =	35 grams
1½ ounces =	40 grams
2½ ounces =	70 grams
4 ounces =	112 grams
5 ounces =	140 grams
8 ounces =	228 grams
10 ounces =	280 grams
15 ounces =	425 grams
16 ounces (1 pound) =	454 grams

Glossary

Aerate: A synonym for sift; to pass ingredients through a fine-mesh device to break up large pieces and incorporate air into ingredients to make them lighter.

Al dente: "To the tooth," in Italian. The pasta is cooked just enough to maintain a firm, chewy texture.

Baste: To brush or spoon liquid fat or juices over meat during roasting to add flavor and prevent drying out.

Bias-slice: To slice a food crosswise at a 45-degree angle.

Bind: To thicken a sauce or hot liquid by stirring in ingredients such as eggs, flour, butter, or cream until it holds together.

Bittersweet Chocolate: is chocolate liquor (or unsweetened chocolate) to which some sugar (typically a third), more cocoa butter, vanilla, and sometimes lecithin has been added. It has less sugar and more liquor than semi-sweet chocolate, but the two are interchangeable in baking. Bittersweet and semi-sweet chocolates are sometimes referred to as "couverture" (chocolate that contains at least 32% cocoa butter); many brands now print on the package the percentage of cocoa (as chocolate liquor and added cocoa butter) contained. The rule is that the higher the percentage of cocoa, the less sweet the chocolate will be.

Blackened: Popular Cajun-style cooking method. Seasoned foods are cooked over high heat in a super-heated heavy skillet until charred.

Blanch: To scald, as in vegetables being prepared for freezing; as in almonds so as to remove skins.

Blend: To mix or fold two or more ingredients together to obtain equal distribution throughout the mixture.

Braise: To brown meat in oil or other fat and then cook slowly in liquid. The effect of braising is to tenderize the meat.

Bread: To coat food with crumbs (usually with soft or dry bread crumbs), sometimes seasoned.

Brown: To quickly sauté, broil, or grill either at the beginning or at the end of meal preparation, often to enhance flavor, texture, or eye appeal.

Brush: To use a pastry brush to coat a food such as meat or pastry with melted butter, glaze, or other liquid.

Butterfly: To cut open a food such as pork chops down the center without cutting all the way through, and then spread apart.

Caramelization: Browning sugar over a flame, with or without the addition of some water to aid the process. The temperature range in which sugar caramelizes is approximately 320 to 360 degrees F.

Chocolate Liquor: The ground up center (nib) of the cocoa bean (otherwise known as unsweetened chocolate).

Clarify: To remove impurities from butter or stock by heating the liquid, then straining or skimming it.

Cocoa Beans: Seeds from the pod of a Theobroma tree. Native to the tropical Amazon forests.

Cocoa Butter: The fat of the cocoa bean.

Cocoa Powder: The cocoa solids resulting from pressing cocoa butter out of chocolate liquor. It is available in different fat levels. It may be natural or dutched.

Coddle: A cooking method in which foods (such as eggs) are put in separate containers and placed in a pan of simmering water for slow, gentle cooking.

Conche: A machine in which the chocolate is kept under constant agitation. This assists in achieving desirable flavors and liquefying the refined chocolate mass.

Confit: To slowly cook pieces of meat in their own gently rendered fat.

Core: To remove the inedible center of fruits such as pineapples.

Couverture: is a term used for chocolates rich in cocoa butter. Popular brands of couverture used by professional pastry chefs and often sold in gourmet and specialty food stores include: Valrhona, Felchlin, Lindt & Sprüngli, Scharffen Berger, Cacao Barry, Callebaut, and Guittard. These chocolates contain a high percentage of cocoa (sometimes 70% or more) and have a total fat content of 30 to 40%.

Cream: To beat vegetable shortening, butter, or margarine, with or without sugar, until light and fluffy. This process traps in air bubbles, later used to create height in cookies and cakes.

Crimp: To create a decorative edge on a pie crust. On a double pie crust, this also seals the edges together.

Curd: A custard-like pie or tart filling flavored with juice and zest of citrus fruit, usually lemon, although lime and orange may also be used.

Curdle: To cause semisolid pieces of coagulated protein to develop in food, usually as a result of the addition of an acid substance, or the overheating of milk or egg-based sauces.

Custard: A mixture of beaten egg, milk, and possibly other ingredients such as sweet or savory flavorings, which are cooked with gentle heat, often in a water bath or double boiler. As pie filling, the custard is frequently cooked and chilled before being layered into a baked crust.

Deglaze: To add liquid to a pan in which foods have been fried or roasted, in order to dissolve the caramelized juices stuck to the bottom of the pan.

Dot: To sprinkle food with small bits of an ingredient such as butter to allow for even melting.

Dredge: To sprinkle lightly and evenly with sugar or flour. A dredger has holes pierced on the lid to sprinkle evenly.

Drippings: The liquids left in the bottom of a roasting or frying pan after meat is cooked. Drippings are generally used for gravies and sauces.

Drizzle: To pour a liquid such as a sweet glaze or melted butter in a slow, light trickle over food.

Dust: To sprinkle food lightly with spices, sugar, or flour for a light coating.

Dutch Process: A treatment used during the making of cocoa powder in which cocoa solids are treated with an alkaline solution to neutralize acidity. This process darkens the cocoa and develops a milder chocolate flavor.

Egg Wash: A mixture of beaten eggs (yolks, whites, or whole eggs) with either milk or water. Used to coat cookies and other baked goods to give them a shine when baked.

Emulsion: A mixture of liquids, one being a fat or oil and the other being water based so that tiny globules of one are suspended in the other. This may involve the use of stabilizers, such as egg or custard. Emulsions may be temporary or permanent.

Entrée: A French term that originally referred to the first course of a meal, served after the soup and before the meat courses. In the United States, it refers to the main dish of a meal.

Fat Bloom: The result of inadequate tempering or temperature abuse of a properly tempered chocolate. It is visible as a dull white film on the surface of the chocolate with the possibility of a soft or crumbling texture on the interior. The product is safe to use.

Fillet: To remove the bones from meat or fish for cooking.

Filter: To remove lumps, excess liquid, or impurities by passing through paper or cheesecloth.

Firm-Ball Stage: In candy making, the point at which boiling syrup dropped in cold water forms a ball that is compact yet gives slightly to the touch.

Flambé: To ignite a sauce or other liquid so that it flames.

Flan: An open pie filled with sweet or savory ingredients; also, a Spanish dessert of baked custard covered with caramel.

Flute: To create a decorative scalloped or undulating edge on a pie crust or other pastry.

Fricassee: Usually a stew in which the meat is cut up, lightly cooked in butter, and then simmered in liquid until done.

Frizzle: To cook thin slices of meat in hot oil until crisp and slightly curly.

Ganache: A rich chocolate filling or coating made with chocolate, vegetable shortening, and possibly heavy cream. It can coat cakes or cookies, and be used as a filling for truffles.

Glaze: A liquid that gives an item a shiny surface. Examples are fruit jams that have been heated or chocolate thinned with melted vegetable shortening. Also, to cover a food with such a liquid.

Gratin: To bind together or combine food with a liquid such as cream, milk, béchamel sauce, or tomato sauce, in a shallow dish. The mixture is then baked until cooked and set.

Hard-Ball Stage: In candy making, the point at which syrup has cooked long enough to form a solid ball in cold water.

Hull (also husk): To remove the leafy parts of soft fruits, such as strawberries or blackberries.

Infusion: To extract flavors by soaking them in liquid heated in a covered pan. The term also refers to the liquid resulting from this process.

Jerk or Jamaican Jerk Seasoning: A dry mixture of various spices such as chilies, thyme, garlic, onions, and cinnamon or cloves used to season meats such as chicken or pork.

Julienne: To cut into long, thin strips.

Jus: The natural juices released by roasting meats.

Larding: To inset strips of fat into pieces of meat, so that the braised meat stays moist and juicy.

Lecithin: A natural emulsifier used in chocolate to improve its flow properties.

Marble: To gently swirl one food into another.

Marinate: To combine food with aromatic ingredients to add flavor.

Meringue: Egg whites beaten until they are stiff, then sweetened. It can be used as the topping for pies or baked as cookies.

Milk Chocolate: Chocolate with at least 10% chocolate liquor and 12% milk solids, combined with sugar, cocoa butter, lecithin, and vanilla.

Mull: To slowly heat cider with spices and sugar.

Nib: The center (meat) of the cocoa bean. When ground, the nib becomes chocolate liquor.

Parboil: To partly cook in a boiling liquid.

Peaks: The mounds made in a mixture. For example, egg white that has been whipped to stiffness. Peaks are "stiff" if they stay upright or "soft" if they curl over.

Pesto: A sauce usually made of fresh basil, garlic, olive oil, pine nuts, and cheese. The ingredients are finely chopped and then mixed, uncooked, with pasta. Generally, the term refers to any uncooked sauce made of finely chopped herbs and nuts.

Pipe: To force a semisoft food through a bag (either a pastry bag or a plastic bag with one corner cut off) to decorate food.

Pressure Cooking: To cook using steam trapped under a locked lid to produce high temperatures and achieve fast cooking time.

Purée: To mash or sieve food into a thick liquid.

Ramekin: A small baking dish used for individual servings of sweet and savory dishes.

Reduce: To cook liquids down so that some of the water evaporates.

Refresh: To pour cold water over freshly cooked vegetables to prevent further cooking and to retain color.

Roux: A cooked paste usually made from flour and butter used to thicken sauces.

Sauté: To cook foods quickly in a small amount of oil in a skillet or sauté pan over direct heat.

Scald: To heat a liquid, usually a dairy product, until it almost boils.

Sear: To seal in a meat's juices by cooking it quickly using very high heat.

Seize: To form a thick, lumpy mass when melted (usually applies to chocolate).

Semi-Sweet Chocolate: is often used for cooking purposes. It is a dark chocolate with a low (typically half) sugar content.

Sift: To remove large lumps from a dry ingredient such as flour or confectioners' sugar by passing it through a fine mesh. This process also incorporates air into the ingredients, making them lighter.

Simmer: To cook food in a liquid at a low enough temperature that small bubbles begin to break the surface.

Steam: To cook over boiling water in a covered pan, this method keeps foods' shape, texture, and nutritional value intact better than methods such as boiling.

Steep: To soak dry ingredients (tea leaves, ground coffee, herbs, spices, etc.) in liquid until the flavor is infused into the liquid.

Stewing: To brown small pieces of meat, poultry, or fish, then simmer them with vegetables or other ingredients in enough liquid to cover them, usually in a closed pot on the stove, in the oven, or with a slow cooker.

Sugar Bloom: Visible as a dull white film on the surface of the chocolate. Dry and hard to the touch, sugar bloom is the result of surface moisture dissolving sugar in the chocolate and subsequent recrystallization of the sugar on the chocolate surface. This is a visual and textural defect.

Sweet Chocolate: Chocolate that contains a minimum of 15% chocolate liquor with varying amounts of sweeteners and cocoa butter.

Tempering: A process of preparing chocolate that involves heating and cooling so that it will solidify with a stable cocoa butter crystal form. Proper tempering, followed by good cooling, is required for good surface gloss and to prevent "fat" bloom.

Thin: To reduce a mixture's thickness with the addition of more liquid.

Truss: To use string, skewers, or pins to hold together a food to maintain its shape while it cooks (usually applied to meat or poultry).

Unleavened: Baked goods that contain no agents to give them volume, such as baking powder, baking soda, or yeast.

Unsweetened chocolate: is pure chocolate liquor, also known as bitter or baking chocolate, mixed with some form of fat to produce a solid substance.

Vinaigrette: A general term referring to any sauce made with vinegar, oil, and seasonings.

Viscosity: The measure of the flow characteristics of a melted chocolate.

White Chocolate: A blend of cocoa butter, milk, sugar, and flavor. Not really "chocolate" since no chocolate solids other than cocoa butter are present. Similar to milk chocolate in composition.

Zest: The thin, brightly colored outer part of the rind of citrus fruits. It contains volatile oils, used as a flavoring.

Recipe Index of Chocolate Delights, Vol. I

315

Reader Feedback Form

Dear Reader,

We are very interested in what our readers think. Please fill in the form below and return it to:

Whispering Pine Press International, Inc.
c/o Chocolate Delights
P.O. Box 214, Spokane Valley, WA 99037-0214
Phone: (509) 928-8700 | Fax: (509) 922-9949
Email: sales@whisperingpinepress.com
Publisher Websites: www.WhisperingPinePress.com
www.WhisperingPinePressBookstore.com
Blog: www.WhisperingPinePressBlog.com

Name: _____

Address: _____

City, St., Zip: _____

Phone/Fax: (____) _____ / (____) _____

Email: _____

Comments/Suggestions: _____

_____

_____

_____

_____

A great deal of care and attention has been exercised in the creation of this book. Designing a great cookbook that is original, fun, and easy to use has been a job that required many hours of diligence, creativity, and research. Although we strive to make this book completely error free, errors and discrepancies may not be completely excluded. If you come across any errors or discrepancies, please make a note of them and send them to our publishing office. We are constantly updating our manuscripts, eliminating errors, and improving quality.

Please contact us at the address above.

About the Cookbook Delights Series

The *Cookbook Delights Series* includes many different topics and themes. If you have a passion for food and wish to know more information about different foods, then this series of cookbooks will be beneficial to you. Each book features a different type of food, such as avocados, strawberries, huckleberries, salmon, vegetarian, lentils, almonds, cherries, coconuts, lemons, and many, many more.

The *Cookbook Delights Series* not only includes cookbooks about individual foods but also includes several holiday-themed cookbooks. Whatever your favorite holiday may be, chances are we have a cookbook with recipes designed with that holiday in mind. Some examples include *Halloween Delights, Thanksgiving Delights, Christmas Delights, Valentine Delights, Mother's Day Delights, St. Patrick's Day Delights,* and *Easter Delights.*

Each cookbook is designed for easy use and is organized into alphabetical sections. Over 250 recipes are included along with other interesting facts, folklore, and history of the featured food or theme. Each book comes with a beautiful full-color cover, ordering information, and a list of other upcoming books in the series.

Note cards, bookmarks, and a daily journal have been printed and are available to go along with each cookbook. You may view the entire line of cookbooks, journals, cards, posters, puzzles, and bookmarks by visiting our websites at www.whisperingpinepress-bookstore.com

and www.chocolatedelights.us, or you can email us with your questions and your comments to: sales@whisperingpinepress.com.

Please ask your local bookstore to carry these sets of books.

To order, please contact:

Whispering Pine Press International, Inc.
c/o Chocolate Delights
P.O. Box 214, Spokane Valley, WA 99037-0214
Phone: (509) 928-8700 | Fax: (509) 922-9949
Email: sales@whisperingpinepress.com
Publisher Websites: www.WhisperingPinePress.com
www.WhisperingPinePressBookstore.com
Blog: www.WhisperingPinePressBlog.com
SAN 253-200X

We Invite You to Join the Whispering Pine Press International, Inc., Book Club!

Whispering Pine Press International, Inc.
c/o Chocolate Delights
P.O. Box 214, Spokane Valley, WA 99037-0214
Phone: (509) 928-8700 | Fax: (509) 922-9949
Email: sales@whisperingpinepress.com
Publisher Websites: www.WhisperingPinePress.com
www.WhisperingPinePressBookstore.com
Blog: www.WhisperingPinePressBlog.com

Buy 11 books and get the next one free, based on the average price of the first eleven purchased.

How the club works:

Simply use the order form below and order books from our catalog. You can buy just one at a time or all eleven at once. After the first eleven books are purchased, the next one is free. Please add shipping and handling as listed on this form. There are no purchase requirements at any time during your membership. Free book credit is based on the average price of the first eleven books purchased.

Join today! Pick your books and mail in the form today!

Yes! I want to join the Whispering Pine Press International, Inc., Book Club! Enroll me and send the books indicated below.

Title   Price

1. _____
2. _____
3. _____
4. _____
5. _____
6. _____
7. _____
8. _____
9. _____
10. _____
11. _____

Free Book Title: _____

Free Book Price: _____ Avg. Price: _____ Total Price: _____

Credit for the free book is based on the average price of the first 11 books purchased.

(Circle one) Check | Visa | MasterCard | Discover | American Express

Credit Card #: _____ Expiration Date: _____

Name: _____

Address: _____

City: _____ State: _____ Country: _____

Zip/Postal: _____ Phone: (_____) _____

Email: _____

Signature_____

Whispering Pine Press International, Inc. Fundraising Opportunities

Fundraising cookbooks are proven moneymakers and great keepsake providers for your group. Whispering Pine Press International, Inc., offers a very special personalized cookbook fundraising program that encourages success to organizations all across the USA.

Our prices are competitive and fair. Currently, we offer a special of 100 books with many free features and excellent customer service. Any purchase you make is guaranteed first-rate.

Flexibility is not a problem. If you have special needs, we guarantee our cooperation in meeting each of them. Our goal is to create a cookbook that goes beyond your expectations. We have the confidence and a record that promises continual success.

Another great fundraising program is the *Cookbook Delights Series* Program. With cookbook orders of 50 copies or more, your organization receives a huge discount, making for a prompt and lucrative solution.

We also specialize in assisting group fundraising – Christian, community, nonprofit, and academic among them. If you are struggling for a new idea, something that will enhance your success and broaden your appeal, Whispering Pine Press International, Inc., can help.

For more information, write, phone, or fax to:

Whispering Pine Press International, Inc.
P.O. Box 214
Spokane Valley, WA 99037-0214
Phone: (509) 928-8700 | Fax: (509) 922-9949
Email: sales@whisperingpinepress.com
Publisher Websites: www.WhisperingPinePress.com
www.WhisperingPinePressBookstore.com
Blog: www.WhisperingPinePressBlog.com
Book Website: www.ChocolateDelights.us
SAN 253-200X

Personalized and/or Translated Order Form for Any Book by Whispering Pine Press International, Inc.

Dear Readers:

If you or your organization wishes to have this book or any other of our books personalized, we will gladly accommodate your needs. For instance, if you would like to change the names of the characters in a book to the names of the children in your family or Sunday school class, we would be happy to work with you on such a project. We can add more information of your choosing and customize this book especially for your family, group, or organization.

We are also offering an option of translating your book into another language. Please fill out the form below telling us exactly how you would like us to personalize your book.

Please send your request to:

Whispering Pine Press International, Inc.
P.O. Box 214, Spokane Valley, WA 99037-0214
Phone: (509) 928-8700 | Fax: (509) 922-9949
Email: sales@whisperingpinepress.com
Publisher Websites: www.WhisperingPinePress.com
www.WhisperingPinePressBookstore.com
Blog: www.WhisperingPinePressBlog.com

Person/Organization placing request: _____

Date_____ Phone: (___) _____

Address_____ Fax: (___) _____

City_____ State_____ Zip: _____

Language of the book: _____

Please explain your request in detail: _____

_____

_____

_____

_____

_____

Chocolate Delights
A Collection of Chocolate Recipes

How to Order

Get your additional copies of this book by returning an order form and your check, money order, or credit card information to:

Whispering Pine Press International, Inc.
P.O. Box 214, Spokane Valley, WA 99037-0214
Phone: (509) 928-8700 | Fax: (509) 922-9949
Email: sales@whisperingpinepress.com
Publisher Websites: www.WhisperingPinePress.com
www.WhisperingPinePressBookstore.com
Blog: www.WhisperingPinePressBlog.com

Customer Name: _____

Address: _____

City, St., Zip: _____

Phone/Fax: _____

Email: _____

- -

Please send me _____ copies of _____
_____ at $_____ per copy
and $4.95 for shipping and handling per book, plus $2.95 each for additional books. Enclosed is my check, money order, or charge my account for $_____.

☐ Check   ☐ Money Order   ☐ Credit Card

(*Circle One*) MasterCard | Discover | Visa | American Express
☐☐☐☐   ☐☐☐☐   ☐☐☐☐   ☐☐☐☐

Expiration Date: _____

_____
Signature

_____
Print Name

Whispering Pine Press International, Inc.
Your Northwest Book Publishing Company
P.O. Box 214
Spokane Valley, WA 99037-0214 USA
Phone: (509) 928-8700 | Fax: (509) 922-9949
Email: sales@whisperingpinepress.com
Publisher Websites: www.WhisperingPinePress.com
www.WhisperingPinePressBookstore.com

Shop Online:
www.whisperingpinepressbookstore.com
Fax orders to: (509)922-9949

Gift-wrapping, Autographing, and Inscription
We are proud to offer personal autographing by the author. For a limited time this service is absolutely free!
Gift-wrapping is also available for $4.95 per item.

1. Sold To

Name: _____
Street/Route: _____
_____
City: _____
State: _____ Zip: _____
Country: _____
Gift message: _____
_____
Email address: _____
Daytime Phone: (__ __) __ __ - __ __ __ __
*Necessary for verifying orders
Home Phone: (__ __) __ __ - __ __ __ __
Fax: (__ __) __ __ - __ __ __ __

2. Ship To

☐ Is this a new or corrected address?
☐ Alternative Shipping Address
☐ Mailing Address

Name: _____
Address: _____
_____
City: _____
State: _____ Zip: _____
Country: _____
Email address: _____

3. Items Ordered

ISBN # /Item #	Size	Color	Qty.	Title or Description	Price	Total

4. Method Of Payment

☐ Visa ☐ MasterCard ☐ Discover ☐ American Express
☐ Check/Money Order Please make it payable to Whispering Pine Press International, Inc. (No Cash or COD's)

Expiration Date

Account Number ____ / ____
                Month Year

☐☐☐☐ ☐☐☐☐ ☐☐☐☐ ☐☐☐☐

Signature_____
            Cardholder's signature
Printed Name_____
            Please print name of cardholder
Address of Cardholder_____
_____

5. Shipping & Handling

Continental US
US Postal Ground: For books please add $4.95 for the first book and $2.95 each for additional books. All non-book items, add 15% of the Subtotal. Please allow 1-4 weeks for delivery.
US Postal Air: Please add $15.00 shipping and handling. Please allow 1-3 days for delivery.

Alaska, Hawaii, and the US Territories
By Ship: Please add 10% shipping and handling (minimum charge $15.00). Please allow 6-12 weeks for delivery.
By Air: Please add 12% shipping and handling (minimum charge $15.00). Please allow 2-6 weeks for delivery.

International
By Ship: Please add 10% shipping and handling (minimum charge $15.00). Please allow 6-12 weeks for delivery.
By Air: Please add 12% shipping and handling (minimum charge $15.00). Please allow 2-6 weeks for delivery.
FedEx Shipments: Add $5.00 to the above airmail charges for overnight delivery.

Subtotal	
Gift wrap $4.95 Each	
For delivery in WA add 8.7% sales tax.	
Shipping See chart at left	
6. Total	

About the Author and Cook

Karen Jean Matsko Hood has always enjoyed cooking, baking, and experimenting with recipes. At this time Hood is working to complete a series of cookbooks that blends her skills and experience in cooking and entertaining. Hood entertains large groups of people and especially enjoys designing creative menus with holiday, international, ethnic, and regional themes.

Hood is publishing a cookbook series entitled the Cookbook Delights Series, in which each cookbook emphasizes a different food ingredient or theme. The first cookbook in the series is Apple Delights Cookbook. Hood is working to complete another series of cookbooks titled Hood and Matsko Family Cookbooks, which includes many recipes handed down from her family heritage and others that have emerged from more current family traditions. She has been invited to speak on talk radio shows on various topics, and favorite recipes from her cookbooks have been prepared on local television programs.

Hood was born and raised in Great Falls, Montana. As an undergraduate, she attended the College of St. Benedict in St. Joseph, Minnesota, and St. John's University in Collegeville, Minnesota. She attended the University of Great Falls in Great Falls, Montana. Hood received a B.S. Degree in Natural Science from the College of St. Benedict and minored in both Psychology and Secondary Education. Upon her graduation, Hood and her husband taught science and math on the island of St. Croix in the U.S. Virgin Islands. Hood has completed postgraduate classes at the University of Iowa in Iowa City, Iowa. In May 2001, she completed her Master's Degree in Pastoral Ministry at Gonzaga University in Spokane, Washington. She has taken postgraduate classes at Lewis and Clark College on the North Idaho college campus in Coeur d'Alene, Idaho, Taylor University in Fort Wayne, Indiana, Spokane Falls Community College, Spokane Community College, Washington State University, University of Washington, and Eastern Washington University. Hood is working on research projects to complete her Ph.D. in Leadership Studies at Gonzaga University in Spokane, Washington.

Hood resides in Greenacres, Washington, along with her husband, many of her seventeen children, and foster children. Her interests include writing, research, and teaching. She previously has volunteered as a court advocate in the Spokane

323

juvenile court system for abused and neglected children. Hood is a literary advocate for youth and adults. Her hobbies include cooking, baking, collecting, photography, indoor and outdoor gardening, farming, and the cultivation of unusual flowering plants and orchids. She enjoys raising several specialty breeds of animals including Babydoll Southdown, Friesen, and Icelandic sheep, Icelandic horses, bichons frisés, cockapoos, Icelandic sheepdogs, a Newfoundland, a Rottweiler, a variety of Nubian and fainting goats, and a few rescue cats. Hood also enjoys bird-watching and finds all aspects of nature precious.

She demonstrates a passionate appreciation of the environment and a respect for all life. She also invites you to visit her websites:

www.KarenJeanMatskoHood.com
www.KarenJeanMatskoHoodBookstore.com
www.KarenJeanMatskoHoodBlog.com
www.KarensKidsBooks.com
www.KarensTeenBooks.com

www.HoodFamilyBlog.com
www.HoodFamily.com

Author's Social Media
Please Follow the Author on **Twitter:** @KarenJeanHood
Friend her on **Facebook:** Karen Jean Matsko Hood Author Fan Page
Google Plus Profile: Karen Jean Matsko Hood
Pinterest.com/KarenJMHood